HEIRLOOM QUILTS

EDITORIAL STAFF

Vice President and Editor-in-Chief:
   Anne Van Wagner Childs
Executive Director: Sandra Graham Case
Editorial Director: Susan Frantz Wiles
Creative Art Director: Gloria Bearden
Senior Graphics Art Director: Melinda Stout

DESIGN
Design Director:
   Patricia Wallenfang Sowers
Senior Designer: Linda Diehl Tiano

PRODUCTION
Managing Editor: Kristine Anderson Mertes
Technical Writers:
   Sherry Solida Ford, Diane Gillian Johns,
   and Barbara McClintock Vechik
Production Assistant: Sharon Heckel Gillam

EDITORIAL
Managing Editor: Linda L. Trimble
Associate Editor: Terri Leming Davidson
Assistant Editors:
   Tammi Williamson Bradley,
   Robyn Sheffield-Edwards,
   Darla Burdette Kelsay, and
   Andrea Isaac Adams
Copy Editor: Laura Lee Weland

ART
Book/Magazine Graphics Art Director:
   Diane M. Hugo
Senior Graphics Illustrator:
   M. Katherine Yancey
Photography Stylists: Pam Choate,
   Sondra Daniel, Karen Smart Hall,
   Aurora Huston, Christina Tiano Myers,
   and Bridgett Shrum

BUSINESS STAFF

Publisher: Bruce Akin
Vice President, Marketing:
   Guy A. Crossley
Marketing Manager: Byron L. Taylor
Print Production Manager: Laura Lockhart
Vice President and General Manager:
   Thomas L. Carlisle
Retail Sales Director: Richard Tignor
Vice President, Retail Marketing:
   Pam Stebbins

Retail Marketing Director:
   Margaret Sweetin
Retail Customer Services Manager:
   Carolyn Pruss
General Merchandise Manager:
   Russ Barnett
Vice President, Finance:
   Tom Siebenmorgen
Distribution Director: Ed M. Strackbein

Library of Congress Catalog Number 96-78953
Hardcover ISBN 0-8487-1576-4
Softcover ISBN 1-57486-019-4

INTRODUCTION

Generations of quilters have provided us with a legacy of unwritten history, both of our communities and our families. Hundreds of patchwork blocks and appliquéd designs endure, chronicling the milestones and manners of days gone by. Today we cherish these hand-pieced links to the past and yearn to create such treasures for our own children. In that spirit, we present Quick-Method Heirloom Quilts, *a collection of patterns from yesteryear created using the faster and easier techniques of today. Follow our simple instructions to discover up-to-date tools and helpful hints that will make the most of your quilting minutes. Whether you want to honor a new addition to the family, a special friendship, or a timeless tradition, you'll be delighted by the myriad of ideas you'll find. And the skill rating assigned to each of our quilts and wall hangings will help you select the projects that are right for you. We've also included a variety of designer-look coordinates — such as a bath set, throw pillows, window treatments, and other decorative accents — to give you the fun of making quilted items, but in a fraction of the time. May our treasury of classic designs provide the inspiration you need to create your own quilting memories!*

TABLE OF CONTENTS

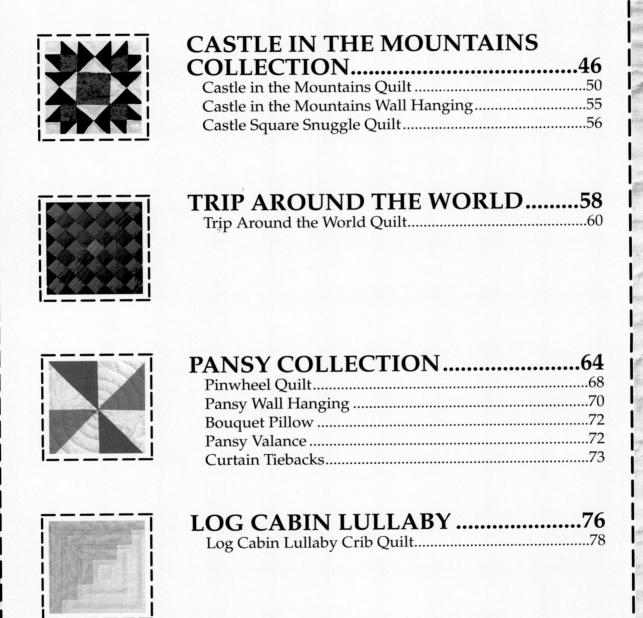

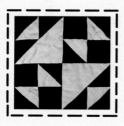

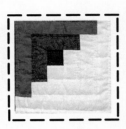

GARDEN WEDDING COLLECTION

A variation of the classic Irish Chain pattern, our Garden Wedding quilt will convey blessings of happiness to the bride and groom. The crisscrossing design, which resembles a trail of stepping stones, is easy to assemble using a variety of strip-pieced units. Symbols of the love that will bloom along the couple's wedded path, the stylized blossoms are made with basic Nine-Patch blocks. To give the illusion of rounded petals, we simply quilted a teardrop pattern inside each sunny square. The leaves are appliquéd using clear nylon thread, so there's no bother with matching thread colors. Presented with our coordinating accessories, this quilt will be an enduring heirloom the newlyweds will cherish.

Atribute to lasting love, this symbolic wall hanging (below) is a heartwarming remembrance of a couple's wedding day. The center motifs are simply fused in place and appliquéd using clear nylon thread. The verse, names, and date are "stitched" on the golden rings using a fabric marking pen. Our charming bath set (opposite) features purchased towels dressed up with pieced borders. The easy-to-make shower curtain valance is abloom with designs from our floral quilt.

GARDEN WEDDING QUILT

SKILL LEVEL: 1 2 3 4 5
QUILT SIZE: 91" x 109"

YARDAGE REQUIREMENTS

Yardage is based on 45"w fabric.

☐ 6¼ yds of cream print
■ 3¼ yds of green print
■ 2¼ yds of pink print
☐ ¾ yd of yellow print
8¼ yds for backing
1 yd for binding
120" x 120" batting

You will also need:
paper-backed fusible web
transparent monofilament thread for appliqué

CUTTING OUT THE PIECES

All measurements include a ¼" seam allowance. Follow
Rotary Cutting, *page 146, to cut fabric unless otherwise*
indicated.

1. **From cream print:** ☐
   - Cut 51 **strips** 2½"w.
   - Cut 6 **wide strips** 3¼"w.
   - Cut 5 strips 4½"w. From these strips, cut 40 **squares** 4½" x 4½".
   - Cut 5 strips 6½"w. From these strips, cut 25 **small rectangles** 2½" x 6½" and 24 **large rectangles** 4½" x 6½".

2. **From green print:** ■
   - Cut 30 **strips** 2½"w.
   - Cut 3 **narrow** strips 1"w.
   - Cut 3 strips 4½"w. From these strips, cut 20 **squares** 4½" x 4½".
   - Use pattern, page 18, and follow **Preparing Fusible Appliqués**, *page 150*, to make 50 **leaf** appliqués.

3. **From pink print:** ■
   - Cut 28 **strips** 2½"w.

4. **From yellow print:** ☐
   - Cut 8 **strips** 2½"w.

ASSEMBLING THE QUILT TOP

Follow **Piecing and Pressing**, *page 148, to make quilt top.*

1. Sew 3 **strips** together to make **Strip Set A**. Make 7 **Strip Set A's**. Cut across **Strip Set A's** at 2½" intervals to make 104 **Unit 1's**.

Strip Set A (make 7) **Unit 1** (make 104)

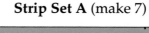

2½"

2. Sew 3 **strips** together to make **Strip Set B**. Make 3 **Strip Set B's**. Cut across **Strip Set B's** at 2½" intervals to make 34 **Unit 2's**.

Strip Set B (make 3) **Unit 2** (make 34)

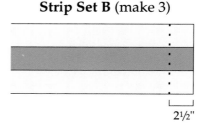

2½"

3. Sew 3 **strips** together to make **Strip Set C**. Make 7 **Strip Set C's**. Cut across 3 **Strip Set C's** at 2½" intervals to make 48 **Unit 3's**. Cut across 2 **Strip Set C's** at 4½" intervals to make 18 **Unit 4's**. Cut across remaining **Strip Set C's** at 6½" intervals to make 22 **Unit 5's**.

Strip Set C (make 7) **Unit 3** (make 48)

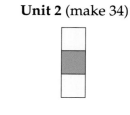

2½"

Unit 4 (make 18) **Unit 5** (make 22)

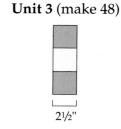

4½" 6½"

4. Sew 3 **strips** together to make **Strip Set D**. Make 3 **Strip Set D's**. Cut across **Strip Set D's** at 2½" intervals to make 48 **Unit 6's**.

Strip Set D (make 3) **Unit 6** (make 48)

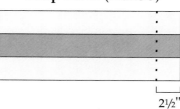

2½"

5. Sew 2 **strips** together to make **Strip Set E**. Make 10 **Strip Set E's**. Cut across **Strip Set E's** at 2½" intervals to make 160 **Unit 7's**.

Strip Set E (make 10) **Unit 7** (make 160)

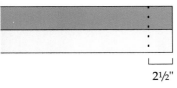

2½"

6. Sew 2 **strips** together to make **Strip Set F**. Make 5 **Strip Set F's**. Cut across **Strip Set F's** at 4½" intervals to make 40 **Unit 8's**.

Strip Set F (make 5) **Unit 8** (make 40)

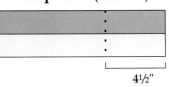

4½"

7. Sew 3 **strips** together to make **Strip Set G**. Make 4 **Strip Set G's**. Cut across **Strip Set G's** at 2½" intervals to make 50 **Unit 9's**.

Strip Set G (make 4) **Unit 9** (make 50)

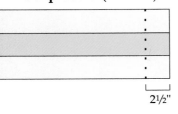

2½"

8. Sew 3 **strips** together to make **Strip Set H**. Make 2 **Strip Set H's**. Cut across **Strip Set H's** at 2½" intervals to make 25 **Unit 10's**.

Strip Set H (make 2) **Unit 10** (make 25)

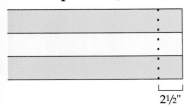

2½"

9. Sew 1 **narrow** and 2 **wide strips** together to make **Strip Set I**. Make 3 **Strip Set I's**. Cut across **Strip Set I's** at 4½" intervals to make 25 **Unit 11's**.

Strip Set I (make 3) **Unit 11** (make 25)

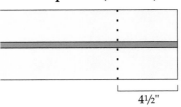

4½"

10. Sew 3 **strips** together to make **Strip Set J**. Make 3 **Strip Set J's**. Cut across **Strip Set J's** at 2½" intervals to make 36 **Unit 12's**.

Strip Set J (make 3) **Unit 12** (make 36)

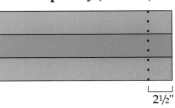

2½"

11. Sew 2 **Unit 1's** and 1 **Unit 2** together to make **Block A**. Make 34 **Block A's**.

Block A (make 34)

12. Sew 2 **Unit 3's**, 2 **Unit 6's**, and 1 **large rectangle** together to make **Block B**. Make 24 **Block B's**.

Block B (make 24)

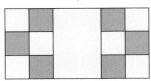

13. Sew 2 **Unit 7's** together to make **Unit 13**. Make 80 **Unit 13's**.

Unit 13 (make 80)

14. Sew 2 **Unit 13's** and 1 **Unit 8** together to make **Unit 14**. Make 40 **Unit 14's**.

Unit 14 (make 40)

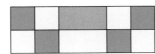

15. Sew 3 **squares** together to make **Unit 15**. Make 20 **Unit 15's**.

Unit 15 (make 20)

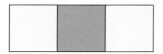

16. Sew 2 **Unit 14's** and 1 **Unit 15** together to make **Block C**. Make 20 **Block C's**.

Block C (make 20)

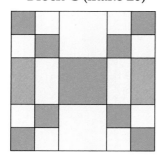

17. Sew 2 **Unit 9's** and 1 **Unit 10** together to make **Unit 16**. Make 25 **Unit 16's**.

Unit 16 (make 25)

18. Sew 1 **small rectangle**, 1 **Unit 16**, and 1 **Unit 11** together to make **Unit 17**. Make 25 **Unit 17's**.

Unit 17 (make 25)

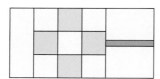

19. Follow **Invisible Appliqué**, page 150, to stitch 2 **leaf** appliqués to 1 **Unit 17** to make **Block D**. Make 25 **Block D's**.

Block D (make 25)

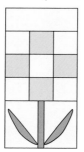

20. Sew 1 **Unit 1** and 1 **Unit 12** together to make **Unit 18**. Make 36 **Unit 18's**.

Unit 18 (make 36)

21. Sew 2 **Unit 18's** and 1 **Unit 4** together to make **Block E**. Make 18 **Block E's**.

Block E (make 18)

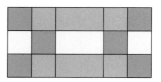

22. Sew 2 **Block A's**, 5 **Unit 5's**, and 4 **Block E's** together to make **Row A**. Make 2 **Row A's**.

Row A (make 2)

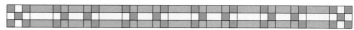

23. Sew 2 **Unit 5's**, 5 **Block A's**, and 4 **Block B's** together to make **Row B**. Make 6 **Row B's**.

Row B (make 6)

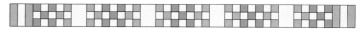

24. Sew 2 **Block E's**, 5 **Block D's**, and 4 **Block C's** together to make **Row C**. Make 5 **Row C's**.

Row C (make 5)

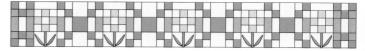

25. Referring to **Quilt Top Diagram**, sew **Rows** together to complete **Quilt Top**.

COMPLETING THE QUILT

1. Follow **Quilting**, page 152, to mark, layer, and quilt using **Quilting Diagram**, page 16, as a suggestion. Our quilt is hand quilted.
2. Cut a 34" square of binding fabric. Follow **Binding**, page 154, to bind quilt using 2½"w bias binding with mitered corners.

Quilting Diagram

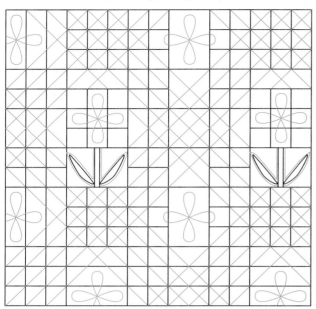

WEDDING DAY WALL HANGING

SKILL LEVEL: 1 2 3 4 5
WALL HANGING SIZE: 22" x 22"

YARDAGE REQUIREMENTS

Yardage is based on 45"w fabric.

- 1/2 yd of green print
- 3/8 yd of cream print
- 1/8 yd of pink print
- 1/8 yd of yellow solid
- scraps of assorted prints for appliqués
  3/4 yd for backing and hanging sleeve
  3/8 yd for binding
  25" x 25" batting

You will also need:
  paper-backed fusible web
  transparent monofilament thread for appliqué
  black permanent fabric pen

CUTTING OUT THE PIECES

*All measurements include a 1/4" seam allowance.
Follow **Rotary Cutting**, page 146, to cut fabric
unless otherwise indicated.*

1. **From green print:**
   - Cut 1 **background** 16" x 16".
   - Cut 8 **squares** 2⅝" x 2⅝".

2. **From cream print:**
   - Cut 2 strips 4¼"w. From these strips, cut 12
     squares 4¼" x 4¼". Cut squares twice
     diagonally to make 48 **triangles**.

3. **From pink print:**
   - Cut 1 strip 2⅝"w. From this strip, cut 8
     squares 2⅝" x 2⅝".

4. **From yellow solid:**
   - Cut 1 strip 2⅝"w. From this strip, cut 8
     squares 2⅝" x 2⅝".

5. **From remaining fabric and scraps:**
   - Referring to photo, use patterns, page 19, and
     follow **Preparing Fusible Appliqués**, page 150,
     to make the following **appliqués**:
     2 **hands** (1 in reverse)   3 **flowers**
     3 **hearts**   3 **flower centers**
     2 **rings**   3 **small leaves**

ASSEMBLING THE WALL HANGING TOP

*Refer to photo and **Wall Hanging Top Diagram** and
follow **Piecing and Pressing**, page 148, to make wall
hanging top.*

1. Use permanent fabric pen to write words on **rings**.
2. Follow **Invisible Appliqué**, page 150, to stitch
   pieces to background. Trim **background** to
   measure 15½" x 15½".
3. Use **triangles** and **squares** to make 4 **Unit 1's**,
   8 **Unit 2's**, 8 **Unit 3's**, and 4 **Unit 4's**.

Unit 1 (make 4)	Unit 2 (make 8)	Unit 3 (make 8)	Unit 4 (make 4)

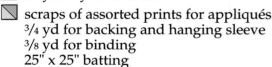

4. Sew 1 **Unit 1**, 2 **Unit 2's**, 2 **Unit 3's**, and 1 **Unit 4**
   together to make **Border Unit**. Make 4
   Border Units.

Border Unit (make 4)

5. Beginning and ending stitching exactly 1/4" from
   each corner of background and backstitching at
   beginning and end of each seam, sew 1 **Border
   Unit** to each edge of **background**.
6. Fold 1 corner of wall hanging top diagonally
   with right sides together, matching outer edges
   of borders. Beginning at point where previous
   seams end, stitch corner seam (**Fig. 1**) to
   complete **Wall Hanging Top**.

Fig. 1

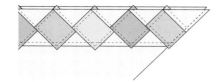

COMPLETING THE WALL HANGING

1. Follow **Quilting**, page 152, to mark, layer, and quilt using **Quilting Diagram** as a suggestion. Our wall hanging is hand quilted.
2. Follow **Making a Hanging Sleeve**, page 156, to attach hanging sleeve.
3. Follow **Binding**, page 154, to bind quilt using 2¹/₂"w straight-grain binding with overlapped corners.

Wall Hanging Top Diagram

Quilting Diagram

SHOWER CURTAIN VALANCE

VALANCE SIZE: 12" x 72"

YARDAGE REQUIREMENTS

Yardage is based on 45"w fabric.

- ³/₄ yd of cream print
- ¹/₂ yd of pink print
- ³/₈ yd of green print
- ¹/₄ yd of yellow print
  1¹/₄ yds for backing and rod pocket

You will also need:
  paper-backed fusible web
  transparent monofilament thread for appliqué

CUTTING OUT THE PIECES

All measurements include a ¹/₄" seam allowance. Follow Rotary Cutting, page 146, to cut fabric unless otherwise indicated.

1. **From cream print:**
   - Cut 6 **strips** 2¹/₂"w. From 1 strip, cut 6 **rectangles** 2¹/₂" x 6¹/₂".
   - Cut 2 **wide strips** 3¹/₄"w.

2. **From pink print:**
   - Cut 4 **strips** 2¹/₂"w.
   - Cut 1 strip 3¹/₂"w. From this strip, cut 2 **side pieces** 3¹/₂" x 12¹/₂".

3. **From green print:**
   - Cut 3 **strips** 2¹/₂"w.
   - Cut 1 **narrow strip** 1"w.
   - Use pattern, page 18, and follow **Preparing Fusible Appliqués**, page 150, to make 12 **leaves**.

4. **From yellow print:**
   - Cut 3 **strips** 2¹/₂"w.

MAKING THE VALANCE

Follow Piecing and Pressing, page 148, to make valance.

1. Follow Steps 1, 3, and 7 - 10 of **Assembling the Quilt Top**, page 12, to make 1 *each* of **Strip Sets A, C, G, H, I,** and **J** and to cut the following **Units:**

10 **Unit 1's**	6 **Unit 10's**
5 **Unit 4's**	6 **Unit 11's**
12 **Unit 9's**	10 **Unit 12's**

2. Follow Steps 17 - 21 of **Assembling the Quilt Top**, page 14, to make 6 **Block D's** and 5 **Block E's**.
3. Referring to photo, sew **side pieces** and **Blocks** together to make **Valance Top**.
4. Cut 1 strip 7" x 72" (pieced as necessary) for rod pocket. Press short edges of strip ¹/₄" to wrong side; press edges ¹/₄" to wrong side again and stitch in place. Press strip in half lengthwise with wrong sides together; baste along long edges to make rod pocket.

5. With right sides together and matching long raw edges, baste rod pocket to upper edge of **Valance Top** (**Fig. 1**).

Fig. 1

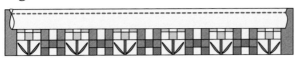

6. Cut valance back same size as **Valance Top**. With right sides together, sew valance top and back together, leaving an opening for turning.
7. Turn valance right side out, carefully pushing corners outward. Blindstitch opening closed. Press rod pocket to back.
8. To secure lower edge of rod pocket, stitch in the ditch through all layers along indicated seamline (**Fig. 2**).

Fig. 2

stitch

TRIMMED TOWELS

Instructions are for trimming 1 bath towel.

YARDAGE REQUIREMENTS
Yardage is based on 45"w fabric.

☐ ¹/₄ yd of cream print

▨ ¹/₈ yd of pink print

▨ scraps of green print and yellow print

You will also need:
  1 bath towel 27" x 50"

CUTTING OUT THE PIECES
All measurements include a ¹/₄" seam allowance. Follow
***Rotary Cutting**, page 146, to cut fabric.*

1. **From cream print:** ☐
   • Cut 4 squares 4¹/₄" x 4¹/₄". Cut squares twice diagonally to make 16 **side triangles**.
   • Cut 2 squares 2³/₈" x 2³/₈". Cut squares once diagonally to make 4 **end triangles**.
2. **From pink print:** ▨
   • Cut 2 **squares** 2⁵/₈" x 2⁵/₈".
   • Cut 2 **borders** 1" x 27¹/₂".
3. **From green print scraps:** ▨
   • Cut 4 **squares** 2⁵/₈" x 2⁵/₈".
4. **From yellow print scraps:** ▨
   • Cut 3 **squares** 2⁵/₈" x 2⁵/₈".

TRIMMING THE TOWELS
*Follow **Piecing and Pressing**, page 148, to trim towels.*

1. Use **side triangles** and **squares** to make 2 **Unit 1's**, 2 **Unit 2's**, and 3 **Unit 3's**.

Unit 1   Unit 2   Unit 3
(make 2)   (make 2)   (make 3)

2. Sew 2 **end triangles**, 1 **side triangle,** and 1 **square** together to make **Unit 4**. Make 2 **Unit 4's**.

Unit 4 (make 2)

3. Referring to **Towel Trim Diagram**, sew units together to make center section of towel trim.
4. Sew **borders** to long edges of center section. Press raw edges ¹/₄" to wrong side to complete **Towel Trim**.

Towel Trim Diagram

5. Referring to photo, position trim on towel and pin or baste in place. Topstitching along pressed edges of trim, sew trim to towel.

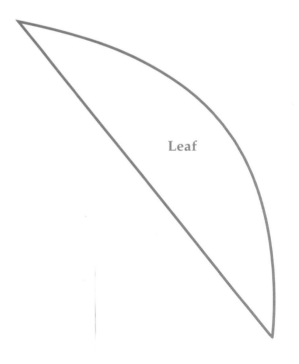

Leaf

Hand

Flower

Flower Center

Heart

Ring

Flower Leaf

19

TRUE LOVER'S KNOT

Pieced in the colors of the heart, the True Lover's Knot pattern is a bold emblem of steadfast devotion. The design is created using two simple templates and small squares for the blocks. Enhanced by strip-set sashing and Nine-Patch sashing squares, the alternating red and white sections create an engaging geometric puzzle. Basic outline quilting enhances the pattern, and the edges are easily finished with bias strip binding. Taken along with a basket lunch and a selection of poetic verses, this gallant spread will be the perfect companion for a romantic picnic in the park!

TRUE LOVER'S KNOT QUILT

SKILL LEVEL: 1 2 3 4 5
BLOCK SIZE: 12" x 12"
QUILT SIZE: 79" x 96"

YARDAGE REQUIREMENTS
Yardage is based on 45"w fabric.

■ 5¹/₂ yds of red solid

☐ 4¹/₄ yds of white solid
7¹/₄ yds for backing
1 yd for binding
90" x 108" batting

CUTTING OUT THE PIECES
All measurements include a ¹/₄" seam allowance. Follow **Rotary Cutting**, *page 146, and* **Template Cutting**, *page 147, to cut fabric.*

1. **From red solid:** ■
   - Cut 36 **strips** 2"w.
   - Cut 6 strips 2"w. From these strips, cut 120 **squares** 2" x 2".
   - Cut 120 **A's** using **Template A** pattern, page 25.
   - Cut 60 **B's** using **Template B** pattern, page 25.

2. **From white solid:** ☐
   - Cut 21 **strips** 2"w.
   - Cut 6 strips 2"w. From these strips, cut 120 **squares** 2" x 2".
   - Cut 120 **A's** using **Template A**.
   - Cut 60 **B's** using **Template B**.

ASSEMBLING THE QUILT TOP
Follow **Piecing and Pressing**, *page 148, to make quilt top.*

1. Sew 1 **A** and 2 **squares** together to make **Unit 1**. Make 60 **Unit 1's**.

Unit 1 (make 60)

2. (**Note:** To sew curved seams in Steps 2 and 3, match centers and pin at center and at each end, then match and pin between pins. Sew seam with convex edge on bottom next to feed dogs.) Sew 1 **A** and 1 **B** together to make **Unit 2**. Make 60 **Unit 2's**.

Unit 2 (make 60)

3. Sew **Unit 1** and **Unit 2** together to make **Unit 3**. Make 60 **Unit 3's**.

Unit 3 (make 60)

4. Repeat Steps 1 - 3 to make 60 **Unit 4's**.

Unit 4 (make 60)

5. Sew 1 **Unit 3** and 1 **Unit 4** together to make **Unit 5**. Make 60 **Unit 5's**.

Unit 5 (make 60)

6. Sew 2 **Unit 5's** together to make **Block**. Make 30 **Blocks**.

Block (make 30)

7. Sew **strips** together to make **Strip Set A**. Make 17 **Strip Set A's**. Cut across **Strip Set A's** at 12¹/₂" intervals to make 49 **Sashing Units**. Cut across remaining **Strip Set A's** at 2" intervals to make 20 **Unit 6's**.

Strip Set A (make 17)

Sashing Unit (make 49)

12¹/₂"

Unit 6 (make 20)

2"

8. Sew **strips** together to make **Strip Set B**. Make 2 **Strip Set B's**. Cut across **Strip Set B's** at 2" intervals to make 40 **Unit 7's**.

Strip Set B (make 2)

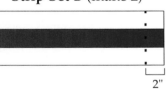

2"

Unit 7 (make 40)

9. Sew 1 **Unit 6** and 2 **Unit 7's** together to make **Unit 8**. Make 20 **Unit 8's**.

Unit 8 (make 20)

10. Sew 5 **Blocks** and 4 **Sashing Units** together to make **Row**. Make 6 **Rows**.

Row (make 6)

11. Sew 5 **Sashing Units** and 4 **Unit 8's** together to make **Sashing Row**. Make 5 **Sashing Rows**.

Sashing Row (make 5)

12. Referring to **Quilt Top Diagram**, page 24, sew **Rows** and **Sashing Rows** together to complete **Quilt Top**.

COMPLETING THE QUILT

1. Follow **Quilting**, page 152, to mark, layer, and quilt using **Quilting Diagram** as a suggestion. Our quilt is hand quilted.
2. Cut a 32" square of binding fabric. Follow **Binding**, page 154, to bind quilt using 2¹/₂"w bias binding with mitered corners.

Quilting Diagram

23

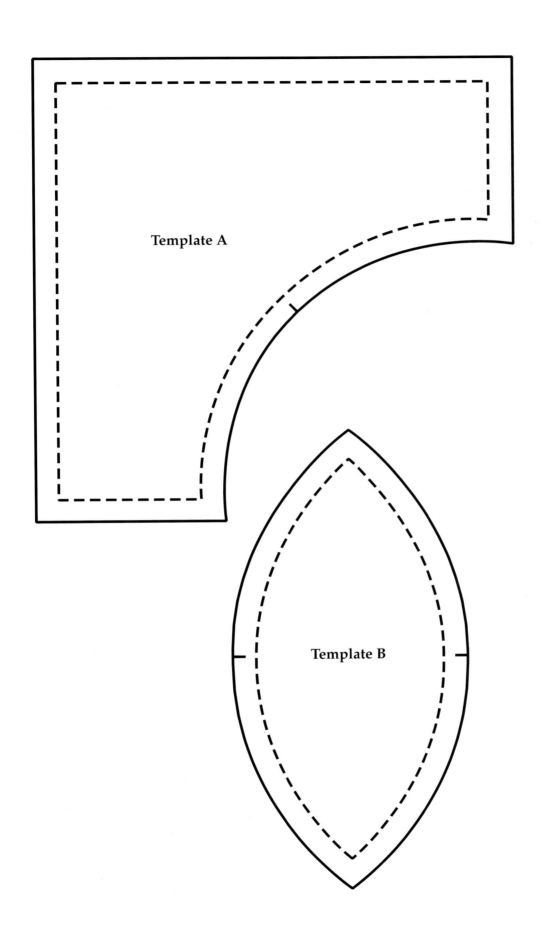

Template A

Template B

FEATHERED STAR COLLECTION

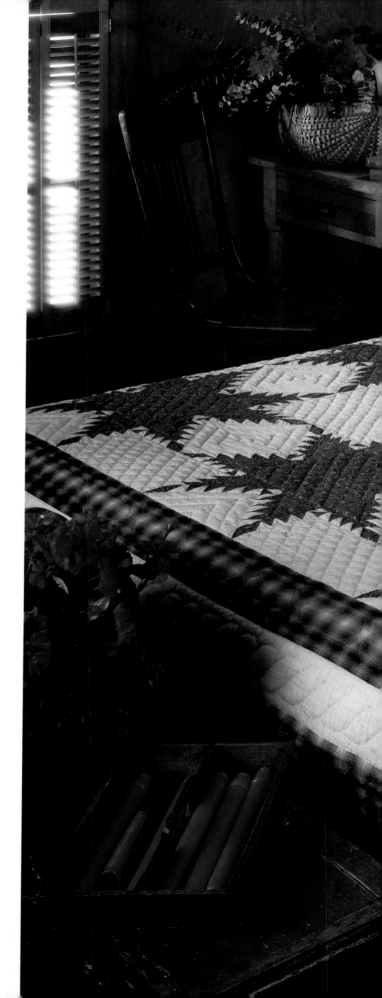

Bursting with provincial blues, this quilt gleams with a constellation of Feathered Stars. The motifs look complex, but they're actually quite simple to piece using plain squares and triangles. Edgings made with easy grid-pieced triangle-squares give each star its radiance. The large celestial designs were set together without sashing, producing a stunning contrast against the creamy background. Plaid inner borders surround the center panel, and a Delectable Mountains border echoes the "rays" of the stars. Complete the stellar look with ruffled pillow shams featuring a variation of the Delectable Mountains pattern.

ighlighted by a dazzling Feathered Star, this decorative throw (opposite)
is enhanced with plain and strip-pieced borders. Simply add a hanging sleeve to
transform it into a beautiful wall hanging. Create a cluster of pretty pillows (below)
for a fun — and fast — way to display your quilting. Coordinating fabrics unite
the designs, which were borrowed from other pattern collections in this volume.

FEATHERED STAR QUILT

SKILL LEVEL: 1 2 3 4 5
BLOCK SIZE: 21¼" x 21¼"
QUILT SIZE: 101" x 105"

YARDAGE REQUIREMENTS
Yardage is based on 45"w fabric.

- ☐ 6⅝ yds of cream print
- 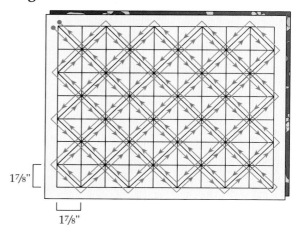 5½ yds of blue print
- ■ 2¾ yds of blue plaid
  9⅛ yds for backing
  1 yd for binding
  120" x 120" batting

CUTTING OUT THE PIECES
All measurements include a ¼" seam allowance. Follow Rotary Cutting, page 146, to cut fabric.

1. **From cream print:** ☐
   - Cut 6 strips 6⅛"w. From these strips, cut 36 **squares** 6⅛" x 6⅛".
   - Cut 2 strips 1⅞"w. From these strips, cut 36 squares 1⅞" x 1⅞". Cut squares once diagonally to make 72 **triangle A's**.
   - Cut 4 strips 2"w. From these strips, cut 72 squares 2" x 2". Cut squares once diagonally to make 144 **triangle B's**.
   - Cut 3 strips 11¼"w. From these strips, cut 9 squares 11¼" x 11¼". Cut squares twice diagonally to make 36 **triangle C's**.
   - Cut 3 strips 10¾"w. From these strips, cut 8 squares 10¾" x 10¾". Cut squares twice diagonally to make 32 **triangle F's**.
   - Cut 2 **rectangles** 15" x 18" for triangle-square A's.
   - Cut 2 squares 10½" x 10½". Cut squares once diagonally to make 4 **corner triangles**.
   - Cut 2 lengthwise strips 3⅞" x 83" for **top/bottom border #2's**.
   - Cut 2 lengthwise strips 3⅞" x 76" for **side border #2's**.
   - Cut 4 **large squares** 20" x 20" for triangle-square B's.

2. **From blue print:**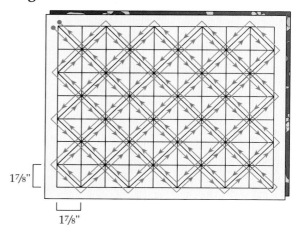
   - Cut 4 **strips** 1½"w.
   - Cut 3 strips 8½"w. From these strips, cut 9 **medium squares** 8½" x 8½".
   - Cut 5 strips 4⅞"w. From these strips, cut 36 squares 4⅞" x 4⅞". Cut squares once diagonally to make 72 **triangle D's**.
   - Cut 2 strips 7⅝"w. From these strips, cut 9 squares 7⅝" x 7⅝". Cut squares twice diagonally to make 36 **triangle E's**.
   - Cut 2 **rectangles** 15" x 18" for triangle-square A's.
   - Cut 1 lengthwise strip 6½" x 105" for **top border #5**.
   - Cut 1 lengthwise strip 3" x 105" for **bottom border #5**.

   - Cut 2 lengthwise strips 3" x 100" for **side border #5's**.
   - Cut 4 **large squares** 20" x 20" for triangle-square B's.

3. **From blue plaid:** ■
   - Cut 2 lengthwise strips 4¼" x 90" for **top/bottom border #3's**.
   - Cut 2 lengthwise strips 4¼" x 83" for **side border #3's**.
   - Cut 2 lengthwise strips 4¼" x 76" for **top/bottom border #1's**.
   - Cut 2 lengthwise strips 4¼" x 68" for **side border #1's**.

ASSEMBLING THE QUILT TOP
Follow Piecing and Pressing, page 148, to make quilt top.

1. To make triangle-square A's, place cream and blue print **rectangles** right sides together. Referring to **Fig. 1**, follow **Making Triangle-Squares**, page 148, to make 126 **triangle-square A's**. Repeat with remaining **rectangles** to make a total of 252 **triangle-square A's**.

Fig. 1

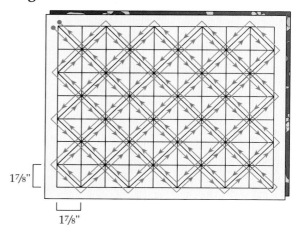

1⅞"

1⅞"

triangle-square A (make 252)

2. To make triangle-square B's, place cream and blue print **large squares** right sides together. Referring to **Fig. 2**, follow **Making Triangle-Squares**, page 148, to make 162 **triangle-square B's**. Repeat with remaining **large squares** to make a total of 648 **triangle-square B's**.

Fig. 2

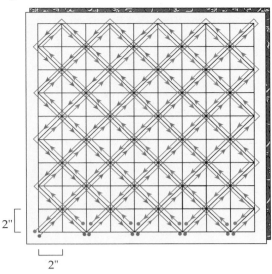

triangle-square B (make 648)

3. To cut diamonds, place 2 **strips** right sides together. Referring to **Fig. 3**, align the 45° marking (shown in pink) on rotary cutting ruler with lower edges of **strips**. Cut along right edge of ruler to cut 1 end of **strips** at a 45° angle.

Fig. 3

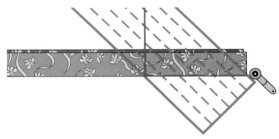

4. Turn cut **strips** 180° on mat and align the 45° marking on ruler with lower edges of **strips**. Align the previously cut 45° edge with the 1⅝" marking on the ruler. Cut **strips** at 1⅝" intervals as shown in **Fig. 4** to cut a total of 36 pairs of **diamonds** (72 **diamonds** total, 36 in reverse).

Fig. 4

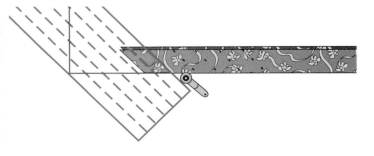

5. Sew 1 **triangle B** and 4 **triangle-square B's** together to make **Unit 1**. Make 4 **Unit 1's**. Sew 1 **triangle B** and 5 **triangle-square B's** together to make **Unit 2**. Make 4 **Unit 2's**.

Unit 1 (make 4)   **Unit 2** (make 4)

6. Sew 1 **triangle C**, 1 **Unit 1**, and 1 **Unit 2** together to make **Unit 3**, leaving portions of seams shown in pink unstitched. Make 4 **Unit 3's**.

Unit 3 (make 4)

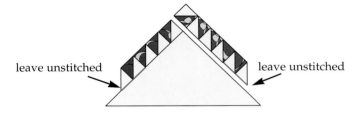

leave unstitched   leave unstitched

7. Sew 1 **Unit 3** and 2 **triangle D's** together to make **Unit 4**. Make 4 **Unit 4's**.

Unit 4 (make 4)

8. Matching shorter side of diamond to **triangle A**, sew 1 **diamond**, 1 **triangle A**, and 3 **triangle-square A's** together to make **Unit 5**. Make 4 **Unit 5's**. Matching shorter side of diamond to **triangle A**, sew 1 reverse **diamond**, 1 **triangle A**, and 4 **triangle-square A's** together to make **Unit 6**. Make 4 **Unit 6's**.

Unit 5 (make 4)   **Unit 6** (make 4)

9. Sew 1 **Unit 5**, 1 **Unit 6**, and 1 **square** together to make **Unit 7**. Make 4 **Unit 7's**.

Unit 7's (make 4)

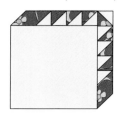

10. Sew **Unit 7's**, **Unit 4's**, and **medium square** together into rows (**Fig. 5**). Sew long seams to join rows, then finish sewing portions of seams left unsewn in Steps 4 and 5 to complete **Block**.

Fig. 5

Block

11. Repeat Steps 5 - 10 to make a total of 9 **Blocks**.
12. Sew 3 **Blocks** together to make **Row**. Make 3 **Rows**.

Row (make 3)

13. Referring to **Quilt Top Diagram**, sew **Rows** together to make center section of quilt top.
14. Follow **Adding Squared Borders**, page 151, to sew **side**, then **top** and **bottom border #1's** to center section. Repeat with **border #2's** and **border #3's**.
15. Sew 4 **triangle-square B's** and 1 **triangle B** together to make **Unit 8**. Make 36 **Unit 8's**. Sew 5 **triangle-square B's** and 1 **triangle B** together to make **Unit 9**. Make 36 **Unit 9's**.

Unit 8 (make 36)   **Unit 9** (make 36)

16. Sew 1 **Unit 8** and 1 **triangle E** together to make **Unit 10**. Make 36 **Unit 10's**.

Unit 10 (make 36)

17. Sew 1 **Unit 9** and 1 **Unit 10** together to make **Unit 11**. Make 36 **Unit 11's**.

Unit 11 (make 36)

18. Sew 9 **Unit 11's** and 8 **triangle F's** together to make **Border #4**. Make 4 **Border #4's**.

Border #4 (make 4)

19. Referring to **Quilt Top Diagram**, sew **Border #4's** then **corner triangles** to center section of quilt top.
20. Follow **Adding Squared Borders**, page 151, to sew **side**, then **top** and **bottom border #5's** to center section to complete **Quilt Top**.

COMPLETING THE QUILT

1. Follow **Quilting**, page 152, to mark layer, and quilt using **Quilting Diagram**, page 34, as a suggestion. Our quilt is hand quilted.
2. Cut a 34" square of binding fabric. Follow **Binding**, page 154, to bind quilt using 2¹/₂"w bias binding with mitered corners.

PILLOW SHAMS

PILLOW SHAM SIZE: 20" x 30" (without ruffle)

Instructions will make 2 pillow shams.

YARDAGE REQUIREMENTS
Yardage is based on 45"w fabric.

☐ 2⁷/₈ yds of cream print

◣ ⁵/₈ yd of blue print

■ ¹/₄ yd of blue plaid
　2 pieces 24" x 34" for sham top backings
　2 pieces 24" x 34" of batting
　2 pieces 7" x 200" for ruffles (pieced as necessary)
　6¹/₄ yds of ¹/₄"w cord for welting
　6¹/₄ yds of 2¹/₂"w bias strip for welting

CUTTING OUT THE PIECES
*All measurements include a ¹/₄" seam allowance unless otherwise specified. Follow **Rotary Cutting**, page 146, to cut fabric.*

1. **From cream print:** ☐
   - Cut 1 strip 2"w. From this strip, cut 12 squares 2" x 2". Cut squares once diagonally to make 24 **small triangles** .
   - Cut 2 **rectangles** 9" x 15" for triangle-squares.
   - Cut 2 **sham centers** 8" x 17¹/₂".
   - Cut 1 square 10⁷/₈" x 10⁷/₈". Cut square twice diagonally to make 4 **large triangles**.
   - Cut 4 squares 10¹/₂" x 10¹/₂". Cut squares once diagonally to make 8 **corner triangles**.
   - Cut 4 **side outer borders** 1¹/₂" x 19¹/₂".
   - Cut 4 **top/bottom outer borders** 1¹/₄" x 31".
   - Cut 4 pieces 21" x 18¹/₂" for **sham backs**.

2. **From blue print:** ◣
   - Cut 1 strip 7⁵/₈"w. From this strip, cut 3 squares 7⁵/₈" x 7⁵/₈". Cut squares twice diagonally to make 12 **medium triangles**.
   - Cut 2 **rectangles** 9" x 15" for triangle-squares.

3. **From blue plaid:** ■
   - Cut 3 strips 1¹/₂"w. From these strips, cut 4 **side inner borders** 1¹/₂" x 8" and 4 **top/bottom inner borders** 1¹/₂" x 19¹/₂".

MAKING THE SHAMS

*Follow **Piecing and Pressing**, page 148, to make pillow shams.*

1. Sew 1 **side inner border** to each short edge of each **sham center**. Sew 1 **top/bottom inner border** to each remaining edge of each **sham center** (**Fig. 1**).

Fig. 1

2. To make triangle-squares, place cream and blue print **rectangles** right sides together. Referring to **Fig. 2**, follow **Making Triangle-Squares**, page 148, to make 56 **triangle-squares**. Repeat with remaining rectangles to make a total of 112 **triangle-squares**. (You will need 108 and have 4 left over.)

Fig. 2

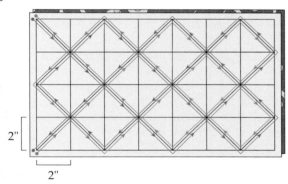

2"

2"

triangle-square (make 112)

3. Sew 4 **triangle-squares** and 1 **small triangle** together to make **Unit 1**. Make 12 **Unit 1's**. Sew 5 **triangle-squares** and 1 **small triangle** together to make **Unit 2**. Make 12 **Unit 2's**.

Unit 1 (make 12)   **Unit 2** (make 12)

4. Sew 1 **Unit 1** and 1 **medium triangle** together to make **Unit 3**. Make 12 **Unit 3's**.

Unit 3 (make 12)

5. Sew 1 **Unit 2** and 1 **Unit 3** together to make **Unit 4**. Make 12 **Unit 4's**.

Unit 4 (make 12)

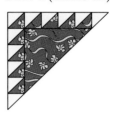

6. Sew 2 **Unit 4's** and 1 **large triangle** together to make **Unit 5**. Make 4 **Unit 5's**.

Unit 5 (make 4)

7. Sew 1 **Unit 4** to each short edge of each **sham center**. Sew 1 **Unit 5** to each long edge of each **sham center** (**Fig. 3**).

Fig. 3

8. Referring to **Sham Top Diagram**, page 36, sew **corner triangles** to **sham centers**. Sew **side**, then **top/bottom outer borders** to each **sham center** to complete 2 **sham tops**.

9. Follow **Quilting**, page 152, to mark, layer, and quilt using **Quilting Diagram**, page 36, as a suggestion. Our **sham tops** are hand quilted.

10. Using a ½" seam allowance, follow **Adding Welting to Pillow Top**, page 157, and **Adding Ruffle to Pillow Top**, page 157, to add welting and ruffle to each **sham top**.

11. On each **sham back** piece, press one 21" edge ½" to the wrong side; press ½" to the wrong side again and stitch in place.

12. To make each sham back, place 2 **sham back** pieces right side up. Referring to **Fig. 4**, overlap finished edges and baste in place.

Fig. 4

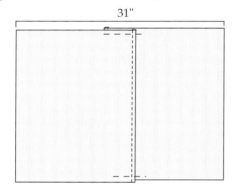

13. To complete each sham, place **sham back** and **Sham Top** right sides together. Stitch through all layers as close as possible to welting. Cut corners diagonally; remove basting threads. Turn shams right side out; press.

Sham Top Diagram

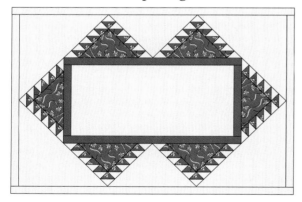

Quilting Diagram

FEATHERED STAR WALL HANGING

SKILL LEVEL: 1 2 3 4 5
BLOCK SIZE: 21¼" x 21¼"
WALL HANGING SIZE: 35" x 35"

YARDAGE REQUIREMENTS

Yardage is based on 45"w fabric.

☐ 1⅛ yds of cream solid
■ 1 yd of blue print
■ ⅝ yd of pink print
1¼ yds for backing and hanging sleeve
½ yd for binding
36" x 36" batting

CUTTING OUT THE PIECES

All measurements include a ¼" seam allowance. Follow Rotary Cutting, page 146, to cut fabric.

1. **From cream solid:** ☐
   - Cut 1 strip 6⅛"w. From this strip, cut 4 **squares** 6⅛" x 6⅛".
   - Cut 3 **wide strips** 2¼"w. Cut strips in half crosswise.
   - Cut 1 **large rectangle** 7" x 13" for triangle-square B's.
   - Cut 1 **rectangle** 5" x 14" for triangle-square A's.
   - Cut 1 square 11¼" x 11¼". Cut square twice diagonally to make 4 **triangle C's**.
   - Cut 4 squares 2" x 2". Cut squares once diagonally to make 8 **triangle B's**.
   - Cut 4 squares 1⅞" x 1⅞". Cut squares once diagonally to make 8 **triangle A's**.
   - Cut 8 **corner squares** 2¼" x 2¼".

2. **From blue print:** ■
   - Cut 2 **strips** 1½"w.
   - Cut 3 **wide strips** 2¼"w. Cut strips in half crosswise.
   - Cut 2 strips 1¼" x 21¾" for **top/bottom border #1's**.
   - Cut 2 strips 1¼" x 23¾" for **side border #1's**.
   - Cut 1 **large rectangle** 7" x 13" for triangle-square B's.
   - Cut 1 **rectangle** 5" x 14" for triangle-square A's.
   - Cut 1 **medium square** 8½" x 8½".
   - Cut 4 squares 4⅞" x 4⅞". Cut squares once diagonally to make 8 **triangle D's**.

3. **From pink print:** ■
   - Cut 2 strips 2¼" x 33¾" for **side border #4's**.
   - Cut 2 strips 2¼" x 30¼" for **top/bottom border #4's**.
   - Cut 4 strips 2¼" x 23¼" for **border #2's**.

ASSEMBLING THE WALL HANGING TOP

*Follow **Piecing and Pressing**, page 148, to make wall hanging top.*

1. To make triangle-square A's, place cream and blue print **rectangles** right sides together. Referring to **Fig. 1**, follow **Making Triangle-Squares**, page 148, to make 28 **triangle-square A's**.

Fig. 1

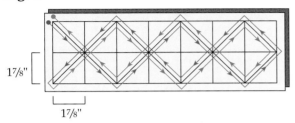

17/8"
17/8"

triangle-square A (make 28)

2. To make triangle-square B's, place cream and blue print **large rectangles** right sides together. Referring to **Fig. 2**, follow **Making Triangle-Squares**, page 148, to make 36 **triangle-square B's**.

Fig. 2

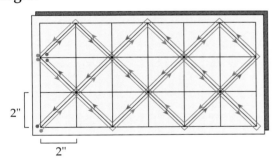

2"
2"

triangle-square B (make 36)

3. Refer to Steps 3 and 4 of **Assembling the Quilt Top**, page 31, to cut 4 pairs of **diamonds** (8 **diamonds** total, 4 in reverse).

4. Follow Steps 5 - 10 of **Assembling the Quilt Top**, page 31, to make **Block**.

5. (*Note:* For Steps 5 - 11, refer to **Wall Hanging Top Diagram**, page 38.) Sew **top** and **bottom**, then **side border #1's** to **Block** to make center section of wall hanging top.

6. Sew 1 **border #2** each to top and bottom edges of center section. Sew 1 **corner square** to each end of remaining **border #2's**; sew borders to side edges of center section.

7. Sew 5 **wide strips** together to make 1 **Strip Set A**. Cut across **Strip Set A** at 2¼" intervals to make **Unit 1**. Make 8 **Unit 1's**.

Strip Set A (make 1)   **Unit 1 (make 8)**

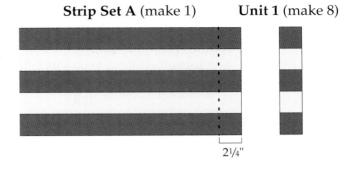

2¼"

8. Sew 5 **wide strips** together to make 1 **Strip Set B**. Cut across **Strip Set B** at 2¼" intervals to make **Unit 2**. Make 4 **Unit 2's**.

Strip Set B (make 1)   **Unit 2 (make 4)**

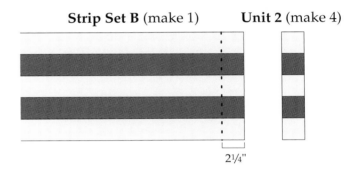

2¼"

9. Sew 2 **Unit 1's** and 1 **Unit 2** together to make **Border #3**. Make 4 **Border #3's**.

Border #3 (make 4)

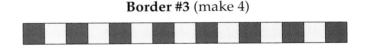

10. Sew 1 **border #3** each to top and bottom of center section. Sew 1 **corner square** to each end of remaining **border #3's**; sew borders to side edges of center section.

11. Sew **top** and **bottom**, then **side border #4's** to center section to complete **Wall Hanging Top**.

COMPLETING THE WALL HANGING

1. Follow **Quilting**, page 152, to mark, layer, and quilt using **Quilting Diagram**, page 38, as a suggestion. Our wall hanging is hand quilted.

2. Follow **Making a Hanging Sleeve**, page 156, to attach hanging sleeve to wall hanging.

3. Follow **Binding**, page 154, to bind wall hanging using 4"w straight-grain binding with overlapped corners.

Wall Hanging Top Diagram

Quilting Diagram

BEAR'S PAW PILLOW

PILLOW SIZE: 10½" x 10½"

YARDAGE REQUIREMENTS

1 fat quarter (18" x 22" piece) *each* of blue print and cream solid
15" x 15" piece for pillow top backing
11" x 11" piece for pillow back
15" x 15" batting

You will also need:
polyester fiberfill

CUTTING OUT THE PIECES

All measurements include a ¼" seam allowance. Follow Rotary Cutting, page 146, to cut fabric.

1. **From blue print:**
    - Cut 1 **medium rectangle** 6" x 11" for triangle-squares.
    - Cut 4 **medium squares** 3½" x 3½".
    - Cut 1 **small square** 2" x 2".

2. **From cream solid:**
    - Cut 1 **medium rectangle** 6" x 11" for triangle-squares.
    - Cut 4 **small rectangles** 2" x 5".
    - Cut 4 **small squares** 2" x 2".

MAKING THE PILLOW

Follow Piecing and Pressing, page 148, to make pillow.

1. Using cream and blue **rectangles**, follow Step 1 of **Assembling the Quilt Top**, page 42, to make 16 **small triangle-squares**.
2. Follow Steps 2 - 8 of **Assembling the Quilt Top**, page 42, to make 1 block for **Pillow Top**.
3. Follow **Quilting**, page 152, to mark, layer, and quilt using **Quilting Diagram** as a suggestion. Our pillow top is hand quilted.
4. Follow **Pillow Finishing**, page 157, to complete pillow.

Pillow Top Diagram   **Quilting Diagram**

GEESE OVER THE MOUNTAIN PILLOW

PILLOW SIZE: 9½" x 9½" (without ruffle)

YARDAGE REQUIREMENTS

1 fat quarter (18" x 22" piece) *each* of pink print, blue print, and cream solid
14" x 14" piece for pillow top backing
10" x 10" piece for pillow back
7" x 76" piece for ruffle (pieced as necessary)
14" x 14" batting

You will also need:
polyester fiberfill

CUTTING OUT THE PIECES

All measurements include a ¼" seam allowance. Follow Rotary Cutting, page 146, to cut fabric.

1. **From pink print:**
    - Cut 1 square 7⅝" x 7⅝". Cut square twice diagonally to make 4 **medium triangles**.

2. **From blue print:**
    - Cut 1 **rectangle** 7" x 13" for triangle-squares.

3. **From cream solid:**
   - Cut 1 **rectangle** 7" x 13" for triangle-squares.
   - Cut 4 **squares** 2" x 2". Cut squares once diagonally to make 8 **small triangles**.

MAKING THE PILLOW

Follow Piecing and Pressing, page 148, to make pillow.

1. Follow Step 2 of **Assembling the Wall Hanging Top**, page 37, to make 36 **triangle-squares**.
2. Follow Steps 3 - 5 of **Making the Shams**, page 35, to make a total of 4 **Unit 4's**. (You will need 4 each of **Unit 1**, **Unit 2**, and **Unit 3**.)
3. Referring to **Pillow Top Diagram**, sew **Unit 4's** together to complete **Pillow Top**.
4. Follow **Quilting**, page 152, to mark, layer, and quilt using **Quilting Diagram** as a suggestion. Our pillow top is hand quilted.
5. Follow **Pillow Finishing**, page 157, to complete pillow with ruffle.

Pillow Top Diagram   **Quilting Diagram**

CROSSES AND LOSSES PILLOW

PILLOW SIZE: 9" x 9" (without ruffle)

YARDAGE REQUIREMENTS

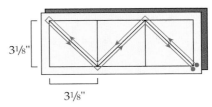 1 fat quarter (18" x 22" piece) *each* of pink print and cream solid
   13" x 13" piece for pillow top backing
   9½" x 9½" piece for pillow back
   1¼ yds of 2"w bias strip for welting
   1¼ yds of ¼" cord for welting
   7" x 72" piece for ruffle (pieced as necessary)
   13" x 13" batting

You will also need:
   polyester fiberfill

CUTTING OUT THE PIECES

All measurements include a ¼" seam allowance. Follow Rotary Cutting, page 146, to cut fabric.

1. **From pink print:**
   - Cut 1 **square** 5⅜" x 5⅜". Cut square once diagonally to make 2 **large triangles**.
   - Cut 1 **rectangle** 5" x 11" for triangle-squares.

2. **From cream solid:**
   - Cut 1 **rectangle** 5" x 11" for triangle-squares.
   - Cut 4 **squares** 2¾" x 2¾".
   - Cut 2 **squares** 3⅛" x 3⅛". Cut squares once diagonally to make 4 **small triangles**.

MAKING THE PILLOW

Follow Piecing and Pressing, page 148, to make pillow.

1. To make triangle-squares, place pink and cream rectangles right sides together. Referring to **Fig. 1**, follow **Making Triangle-Squares**, page 148, to make 6 **triangle-squares**.

Fig. 1

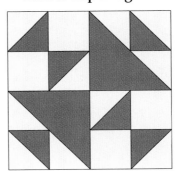

3⅛"

3⅛"

triangle-square (make 6)

2. Follow Steps 2 - 5 of **Assembling the Quilt Top**, page 84, to make 1 **Block** for **Pillow Top**. (You will need 2 each of **Unit 1**, **Unit 2**, and **Unit 3**.)
3. Follow **Quilting**, page 152, to mark, layer, and quilt using **Quilting Diagram** as a suggestion. Our pillow top is hand quilted.
4. Follow **Pillow Finishing**, page 157, to complete pillow with welting and ruffle.

Pillow Top Diagram   **Quilting Diagram**

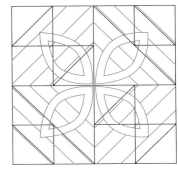

SCRAPPY BEAR'S PAW

A *classic pattern found in many areas of the United States, this quilt block was often titled to reflect the region in which it was made. To quilters on the frontier, who likely faced their share of grizzlies, the design was known as Bear's Paw. Stitchers on Long Island dubbed it Duck's Foot in the Mud in honor of the flocks that resided on the shore. And in the Quaker tradition of the Northeast, Pennsylvanians recognized the pattern as Hand of Friendship. For our Bear's Paw quilt, we used a variety of soft prints and united the scrappy look with pink sashing and a blue print border. Grid-pieced triangle-squares make easy work of the blocks and the sawtooth border.*

SCRAPPY BEAR'S PAW QUILT

SKILL LEVEL: 1 2 3 4 5
BLOCK SIZE: 10½" x 10½"
QUILT SIZE: 94" x 107"

YARDAGE REQUIREMENTS
Yardage is based on 45"w fabric.

■ 3 yds of blue print
▦ 2¾ yds of peach solid
▦ 1¼ yds of blue solid
▢ ⅞ yd of light blue print
◸ 12" x 13" piece *each* of 30 light prints
◣ 12" x 16" piece *each* of 30 dark prints
  8½ yds for backing
  1 yd for binding
  120" x 120" batting

CUTTING OUT THE PIECES
All measurements include a ¼" seam allowance. Follow
Rotary Cutting, page 146, to cut fabric.

1. **From blue print:** ■
   • Cut 2 lengthwise **top/bottom borders** 9½" x 97".
   • Cut 2 lengthwise **side borders** 9½" x 92".

2. **From peach solid:** ▦
   • Cut 24 strips 3½"w. From these strips, cut 71 **sashing strips** 3½" x 11".

3. **From blue solid:** ▦
   • Cut 4 strips 3½"w. From these strips, cut 42 **sashing squares** 3½" x 3½".
   • Cut 2 **large rectangles** 16" x 25" for large triangle-squares.

4. **From light blue print:** ▢
   • Cut 2 **large rectangles** 16" x 25" for large triangle-squares.

5. **From *each* light print:** ◸
   • Cut 1 **medium rectangle** 6" x 11" for small triangle-squares.
   • Cut 4 **small squares** 2" x 2".
   • Cut 4 **small rectangles** 2" x 5".

6. **From *each* dark print:** ◣
   • Cut 1 **medium rectangle** 6" x 11" for small triangle-squares.
   • Cut 1 **small square** 2" x 2".
   • Cut 4 **medium squares** 3½" x 3½".

ASSEMBLING THE QUILT TOP
Follow Piecing and Pressing, page 148, to make quilt top.

1. (*Note:* For each block, choose 1 dark print and 1 light print.) To make small triangle-squares, place 1 light print and 1 dark print **medium rectangle** right sides together.

Referring to **Fig. 1**, follow **Making Triangle-Squares**, page 148, to make 16 **small triangle-squares**.

Fig. 1

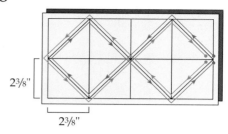

2⅜"
2⅜"

small triangle-square (make 16)

2. Sew 2 **small triangle-squares** together to make **Unit 1**. Make 4 **Unit 1's**. Sew 2 **small triangle-squares** together to make **Unit 2**. Make 4 **Unit 2's**.

Unit 1 (make 4)   **Unit 2** (make 4)

3. Sew 1 **small square** and 1 **Unit 1** together to make **Unit 3**. Make 4 **Unit 3's**.

Unit 3 (make 4)

4. Sew 1 **Unit 2** and 1 **medium square** together to make **Unit 4**. Make 4 **Unit 4's**.

Unit 4 (make 4)

5. Sew 1 **Unit 3** and 1 **Unit 4** together to make **Unit 5**. Make 4 **Unit 5's**.

Unit 5 (make 4)

6. Sew 2 **Unit 5's** and 1 **small rectangle** together to make **Unit 6**. Make 2 **Unit 6's**.

Unit 6 (make 2)

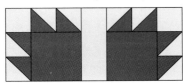

7. Sew 2 **small rectangles** and 1 **small square** together to make 1 **Unit 7**.

Unit 7 (make 1)

8. Sew **Unit 6's** and **Unit 7** together to make **Block**.

Block

9. Repeat Steps 1 - 8 to make a total of 30 **Blocks**.
10. Sew 6 **sashing strips** and 5 **Blocks** together to make **Row**. Make 6 **Rows**.

Row (make 6)

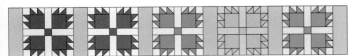

11. Sew 6 **sashing squares** and 5 **sashing strips** together to make **Sashing Row**. Make 7 **Sashing Rows**.

Sashing Row (make 7)

12. Referring to **Quilt Top Diagram**, page 44, sew **Rows** and **Sashing Rows** together to make center section of quilt top.
13. To make large triangle-squares, place 1 blue solid and 1 light blue print **large rectangle** right sides together. Referring to **Fig. 2**, follow **Making Triangle-Squares**, page 148, to make 80 **large triangle-squares**. Repeat with remaining **rectangles** to make a total of 160 **large triangle-squares**. (You will need 158 and have 2 left over.)

Fig. 2

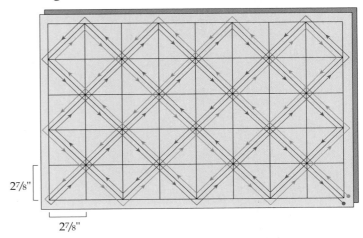

2⅞"

2⅞"

large triangle-square (make 160)

14. Sew 35 **large triangle-squares** together to make **Top/Bottom Sawtooth Border**. Make 2 **Top/Bottom Sawtooth Borders**. Sew 44 **large triangle-squares** together to make **Side Sawtooth Border**. Make 2 **Side Sawtooth Borders**.

Top/Bottom Sawtooth Border (make 2)

Side Sawtooth Border (make 2)

15. Referring to **Quilt Top Diagram**, sew **Top/Bottom Sawtooth Borders** to top and bottom edges of center section, easing in any fullness. Sew **Side Sawtooth Borders** to side edges of center section.
16. Follow **Adding Squared Borders**, page 151, to add **side**, then **top** and **bottom outer borders** to center section to complete **Quilt Top**.

COMPLETING THE QUILT
1. Follow **Quilting**, page 152, to mark, layer, and quilt using **Quilting Diagram** as a suggestion. Our quilt is hand quilted.
2. Cut a 34" square of binding fabric. Follow **Binding**, page 154, to bind quilt using 2½"w bias binding with mitered corners.

Quilt Top Diagram

FITTING A PIECED BORDER

Pieced borders can add wonderful visual interest to your quilt, but with so many pieces and seams, fitting them to your quilt top can be a challenge. Measuring, measuring, and more measuring at critical points will ensure that the quilt top fits together from the center to the very edges.

- Making pieced borders fit begins when cutting and assembling the center section of the quilt top. Be as accurate as possible in your cutting and pay strict attention to consistently making ¼" seams. Finish each step with careful pressing.
- Measure often as you complete the units of the center section of your quilt top to make sure that you are staying on track.

By doing so, you can make adjustments as you go. Measure the size of finished blocks, the length of rows, and the size of other units or sections, so that you will finish with the correct size center section.

- As you add to the center section, measure to be sure that opposite edges (both sides or top and bottom) are remaining equal in length. A perfectly symmetrical center section will need fewer adjustments in the lengths of the borders.
- After completing ¼ or ½ of your pieced border, measure to see how you are doing. Then, if necessary, you can make small adjustments in the remaining seam allowances.

CASTLE IN THE MOUNTAINS COLLECTION

Two old-time quilting favorites — the Castle Keep and Delectable Mountains patterns — combine with contemporary style for our handsome Castle in the Mountains quilt. The block-within-a-block look of the Castle Keep design is produced using grid-pieced units, along with rotary cut triangles and squares. The blocks are set together without sashing for an intriguing arrangement of geometric shapes. A range of Delectable Mountains motifs, made with simple templates, forms a majestic inner border. The soothing, muted shades of the blocks are echoed in the outer borders.

Pieced in rich burgundy and navy, this comfy lap quilt (opposite) is a cuddly companion to our Castle in the Mountains quilt. The Square-Within-a-Square pattern, a traditional Amish design, is created by stitching triangles around a large, plain square. The quilt is assembled with generous sashing strips and finished with Baptist fan quilting. Completing the collection is a splendid wall hanging (below), a scaled-down version of the regal quilt.

CASTLE IN THE MOUNTAINS QUILT

SKILL LEVEL: 1 2 3 4 5
BLOCK SIZE: 18" x 18"
QUILT SIZE: 79" x 97"

YARDAGE REQUIREMENTS
Yardage is based on 45"w fabric.

- 5¼ yds of burgundy print
- 3⅜ yds of navy solid
- 3 yds of tan solid
- 2¾ yds of plaid
- 1⅞ yds of tan print
- ½ yd of dark burgundy print
  7¼ yds for backing
  1 yd for binding
  90" x 108" batting

CUTTING OUT THE PIECES
All measurements include a ¼" seam allowance. Follow
Rotary Cutting, page 146, to cut fabric.

1. **From burgundy print:**
   - Cut 5 strips 3⅞"w. From these strips, cut 48 squares 3⅞" x 3⅞". Cut squares once diagonally to make 96 **triangles**.
   - Cut 2 strips 1½"w. From these strips, cut 48 **small squares** 1½" x 1½".
   - Cut 1 strip 2½"w. From this strip, cut 12 **medium squares** 2½" x 2½".
   - Cut 16 strips 3½"w. From these strips, cut 192 **large squares** 3½" x 3½".
   - Cut 2 lengthwise **side outer borders** 4¾" x 92".
   - Cut 2 lengthwise **top/bottom outer borders** 4¾" x 82".

2. **From navy solid:** ■
   - Cut 14 **strips** 2"w for pieced borders.
   - Cut 2 lengthwise **side inner borders** 1½" x 84".
   - Cut 2 lengthwise **top/bottom inner borders** 1½" x 68".
   - From remaining fabric width, cut 1 **large rectangle** 14" x 21" for large triangle-squares.
   - From remaining fabric width, cut 1 **small rectangle** 13" x 16" for small triangle-squares.

3. **From tan solid:** ☐
   - Cut 20 strips 3½"w. From these strips, cut 96 **rectangles** 3½" x 6½" and 48 **large squares** 3½" x 3½".
   - Cut 2 strips 1½"w. From these strips, cut 48 **small squares** 1½" x 1½".
   - Cut 1 **large rectangle** 14" x 21" for large triangle-squares.
   - Cut 1 **small rectangle** 13" x 16" for small triangle-squares.

4. **From plaid:** ▨
   - Cut 2 lengthwise **side middle borders** 3¼" x 86".
   - Cut 2 lengthwise **top/bottom middle borders** 3¼" x 74".

5. **From tan print:** ▨
   - Cut 14 **strips** 2"w for pieced borders.
   - Cut 4 strips 3½"w. From these strips, cut 48 **large squares** 3½" x 3½".
   - Cut 3 strips 4¼"w. From these strips, cut 24 squares 4¼" x 4¼". Cut squares twice diagonally to make 96 **small triangles**.
   - Cut 4 **corner squares** 4½" x 4½".

6. **From dark burgundy print:** ■
   - Cut 3 strips 4¼"w. From these strips, cut 24 squares 4¼" x 4¼". Cut squares twice diagonally to make 96 **small triangles**.

ASSEMBLING THE QUILT TOP
*Follow **Piecing and Pressing**, page 148, to make quilt top.*
MAKING THE BLOCKS

1. To make small triangle-squares, place tan and navy **small rectangles** right sides together. Referring to **Fig. 1**, follow **Making Triangle-Squares**, page 148, to make 96 **small triangle-squares**.

Fig. 1

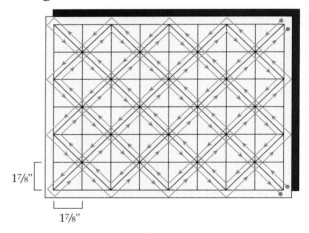

small triangle-square (make 96)

2. Sew 2 **small triangle-squares** and 2 **small squares** together to make **Unit 1**. Make 48 **Unit 1's**.

Unit 1 (make 48)

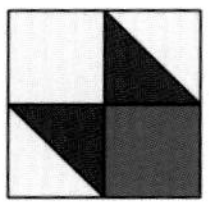

3. To make large triangle-squares, place tan and navy **large rectangles** right sides together. Referring to **Fig. 2**, follow **Making Triangle-Squares**, page 148, to make 48 **large triangle-squares**.

Fig. 2

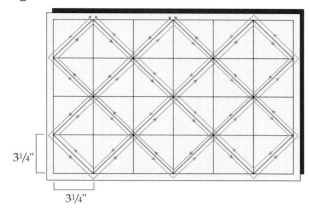

3¼"

3¼"

large triangle-square (make 48)

4. Referring to **Fig. 3**, place 2 **large triangle-squares** right sides and opposite colors together, matching seams. Referring to **Fig. 4**, draw a diagonal line (shown in pink) from corner to corner. Stitch ¼" on both sides of drawn line. Cut on drawn line and press open to make 2 **triangle units**. Repeat with remaining **large triangle-squares** to make a total of 48 **triangle units**.

Fig. 3   **Fig. 4**

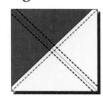

triangle unit (make 48)

5. Sew 2 **Unit 1's** and 1 **triangle unit** together to make **Unit 2**. Make 24 **Unit 2's**.

Unit 2 (make 24)

6. Sew 2 **triangle units** and 1 **medium square** together to make **Unit 3**. Make 12 **Unit 3's**.

Unit 3 (make 12)

7. Sew 2 **Unit 2's** and 1 **Unit 3** together to make **Unit 4**. Make 12 **Unit 4's**.

Unit 4 (make 12)

8. Sew 2 **small triangles** together to make **Unit 5**. Make 48 **Unit 5's**. Sew 2 **small triangles** together to make **Unit 6**. Make 48 **Unit 6's**.

Unit 5 (make 48)   **Unit 6** (make 48)

9. Sew 1 **triangle** and 1 **Unit 5** together to make **Unit 7**. Make 48 **Unit 7's**. Sew 1 **triangle** and 1 **Unit 6** together to make **Unit 8**. Make 48 **Unit 8's**.

Unit 7 (make 48)   **Unit 8** (make 48)

10. Sew 1 **Unit 7** and 1 **Unit 8** together to make **Unit 9**. Make 48 **Unit 9's**.

Unit 9 (make 48)

11. Sew 2 **large squares** and 1 **Unit 9** together to make **Unit 10**. Make 24 **Unit 10's**.

Unit 10 (make 24)

12. Sew 2 **Unit 9's**, 1 **Unit 4**, then 2 **Unit 10's** together to make **Unit 11**. Make 12 **Unit 11's**.

Unit 11 (make 12)

13. Place 1 **large square** on 1 **rectangle** with right sides together and stitch diagonally (**Fig. 5**). Trim 1/4" from stitching line (**Fig. 6**). Press open, pressing seam allowance toward darker fabric.

Fig. 5   **Fig. 6**

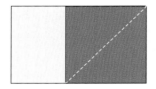   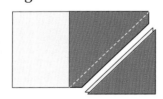

14. Place 1 **large square** on opposite end of **rectangle** and stitch diagonally (**Fig. 7**). Trim and press open as in Step 13 to make **Unit 12**.

Fig. 7   **Unit 12**

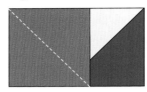 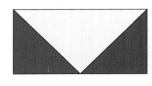

15. Repeat Steps 13 and 14 to make a total of 96 **Unit 12's**.
16. Sew 2 **Unit 12's** together to make **Unit 13**. Make 48 **Unit 13's**.

Unit 13 (make 48)

17. Sew 2 **large squares** and 1 **Unit 13** together to make **Unit 14**. Make 24 **Unit 14's**.

Unit 14 (make 24)

18. Sew 2 **Unit 13's**, 1 **Unit 11**, then 2 **Unit 14's** together to make **Block**. Make 12 **Blocks**.

Block (make 12)

19. Sew 3 **Blocks** together to make **Row**. Make 4 **Rows**.

Row (make 4)

20. Referring to **Quilt Top Diagram**, page 54, sew **Rows** together to make center section of quilt top.

MAKING THE PIECED BORDER
1. Follow Step 1 of **Template Cutting**, page 147, and use patterns, page 57, to make **Templates A, B,** and **C**.
2. Place 2 tan **strips** right sides together. Referring to **Fig. 8**, use **Template A** to mark 28 **A's** on top **strip**. Keeping **strips** stacked together, use rotary cutter and ruler to cut 28 pairs of **A's**. (You will cut 28 **A's** and 28 **reverse A's** from strips). Repeat using navy **strips**.

Fig. 8

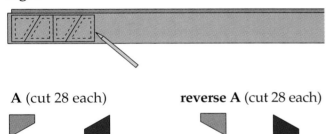

A (cut 28 each)   **reverse A** (cut 28 each)

3. Referring to Step 2, use 3 pairs of tan **strips** and **Template B** to cut a total of 28 **B's** and 28 **reverse B's**. Repeat using navy **strips**.

B (cut 28 each)   **reverse B** (cut 28 each)

4. Referring to Step 2, use 2 pairs of tan **strips** and **Template C** to cut a total of 28 **C's** and 28 **reverse C's**. Repeat using navy **strips**.

C (cut 28 each)   **reverse C** (cut 28 each)

5. Referring to diagrams for color placement, use 1 **A** (tan) and 1 **B** (navy) to make **Unit 15**; use 2 **C's** to make **Unit 16**; use 1 **A** (navy) and 1 **B** (tan) to make **Unit 17**; use 1 **reverse A** (navy) and 1 **reverse B** (tan) to make **Unit 18**; use 2 **reverse C's** to make **Unit 19**; and use 1 **reverse A** (tan) and 1 **reverse B** (navy) to make **Unit 20**. Make 28 each of **Units 15 - 20**.

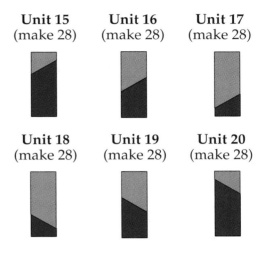

Unit 15   **Unit 16**   **Unit 17**
(make 28)   (make 28)   (make 28)

Unit 18   **Unit 19**   **Unit 20**
(make 28)   (make 28)   (make 28)

6. Sew 1 each of **Unit 15**, **Unit 16**, **Unit 17**, **Unit 18**, **Unit 19**, and **Unit 20** together to make **Border Unit**. Make 28 **Border Units**.

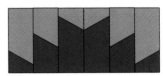

Border Unit (make 28)

7. Sew 8 **Border Units** together to make **Side Pieced Border**. Make 2 **Side Pieced Borders**.

Side Pieced Border (make 2)

8. Sew 2 **corner squares** and 6 **Border Units** together to make **Top/Bottom Pieced Border**. Make 2 **Top/Bottom Pieced Borders**.

Top/Bottom Pieced Border (make 2)

9. Sew **Side**, then **Top** and **Bottom Pieced Borders** to center section of quilt top.
10. Referring to **Quilt Top Diagram**, follow **Adding Squared Borders**, page 151, to add **side**, then **top** and **bottom inner borders**. Repeat to add **middle** and **outer borders** to complete **Quilt Top**.

COMPLETING THE QUILT

1. Follow **Quilting**, page 152, to mark, layer, and quilt using **Quilting Diagram** as a suggestion. Our quilt is hand quilted.
2. Cut a 32" square of binding fabric. Follow **Binding**, page 154, to bind quilt using 2½"w bias binding with mitered corners.

Quilting Diagram

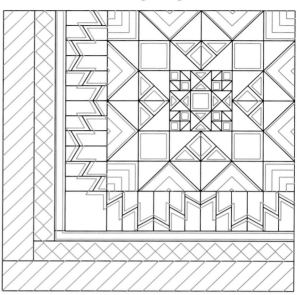

Quilt Top Diagram

CASTLE IN THE MOUNTAINS WALL HANGING

SKILL LEVEL: 1 2 3 4 5
WALL HANGING SIZE: 39" x 39"

YARDAGE REQUIREMENTS

Yardage is based on 45"w fabric.

- ⬛ 7/8 yd of burgundy print
- ⬛ 5/8 yd of navy solid
- ⬛ 1/2 yd of tan print
- ⬛ 3/8 yd of plaid
- ⬛ 1/4 yd of burgundy solid
- ⬜ 1/2 yd of tan solid
  1 5/8 yds for backing and hanging sleeve
  3/8 yd for binding
  42" x 42" batting

CUTTING OUT THE PIECES

All measurements include a 1/4" seam allowance. Follow Rotary Cutting, page 146, to cut fabric.

1. **From burgundy print:** ⬛
   - Cut 4 strips 3 3/8"w for **outer borders**.
   - Cut 2 strips 3 1/2"w. From these strips, cut 16 **large squares** 3 1/2" x 3 1/2".
   - Cut 4 squares 3 7/8" x 3 7/8". Cut squares once diagonally to make 8 **triangles**.
   - Cut 4 **small squares** 1 1/2" x 1 1/2".
   - Cut 1 **medium square** 2 1/2" x 2 1/2".

2. **From navy solid:** ⬛
   - Cut 4 **strips** 2"w for pieced borders.
   - Cut 4 strips 1 1/2"w for **inner borders**.
   - Cut 1 **square** 5" x 5" for small triangle-squares.
   - Cut 1 **large rectangle** 5" x 8" for large triangle-squares.

3. **From tan print:** ⬛
   - Cut 4 **strips** 2"w for pieced borders.
   - Cut 4 **corner squares** 4 1/2" x 4 1/2".
   - Cut 4 **large squares** 3 1/2" x 3 1/2".
   - Cut 2 squares 4 1/4" x 4 1/4". Cut squares twice diagonally to make 8 **small triangles**.

4. **From plaid:** ⬛
   - Cut 4 strips 2 1/2"w for **middle borders**.

5. **From burgundy solid:** ⬛
   - Cut 2 squares 4 1/4" x 4 1/4". Cut squares twice diagonally to make 8 **small triangles**.

6. **From tan solid:** ⬜
   - Cut 2 strips 3 1/2"w. From these strips, cut 8 **rectangles** 3 1/2" x 6 1/2" and 4 **large squares** 3 1/2" x 3 1/2".
   - Cut 1 **large rectangle** 5" x 8" for large triangle-squares.

- Cut 4 **small squares** 1 1/2" x 1 1/2".
- Cut 1 **square** 5" x 5" for small triangle-squares.

ASSEMBLING THE WALL HANGING TOP

Follow Piecing and Pressing, page 148, to make wall hanging top.

1. To make small triangle-squares, place tan and navy **squares** right sides together. Referring to **Fig. 1**, follow **Making Triangle-Squares**, page 148, to make 8 **small triangle-squares**.

Fig. 1

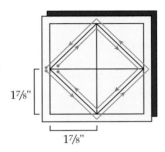

small triangle-square (make 8)

2. Sew 2 **small triangle-squares** and 2 **small squares** together to make **Unit 1**. Make 4 **Unit 1's**.

Unit 1 (make 4)

3. To make large triangle-squares, place tan and navy **large rectangles** right sides together. Referring to **Fig. 2**, follow **Making Triangle-Squares**, page 148, to make 4 **large triangle-squares**.

Fig. 2

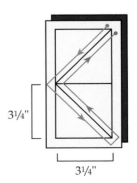

large triangle-square (make 4)

4. Referring to Step 4 of **Assembling the Quilt Top**, page 51, use **large triangle-squares** to make a total of 4 **triangle units**.

5. Referring to Steps 5 - 12 of **Assembling the Quilt Top**, page 51, make 1 **Unit 11**. (You will need 2 **Unit 2's**, 1 **Unit 3**, 1 **Unit 4**, 4 **Unit 5's**, 4 **Unit 6's**, 4 **Unit 7's**, 4 **Unit 8's**, 4 **Unit 9's**, and 2 **Unit 10's**.)

6. Refer to Steps 13 - 18 of **Assembling the Quilt Top**, page 52, to make 1 **Block**. (You will need 1 **Unit 11**, 8 **Unit 12's**, 4 **Unit 13's**, and 2 **Unit 14's**.)

7. Follow Step 1 of **Making the Pieced Border**, page 53, to make **Templates**.

8. Fold 1 tan **strip** in half with right sides together. Referring to Step 2 of **Making the Pieced Border**, page 53, mark and cut 8 **A's** and 8 **reverse A's** from folded strip. Repeat using navy **strip**.

9. Using 2 tan strips, refer to Step 3 of **Making the Pieced Border**, page 53, to cut 8 **B's** and 8 **reverse B's**. Repeat using navy **strips**.

10. Fold remaining tan **strip** in half with right sides together. Referring to Step 4 of **Making the Pieced Border**, page 53, cut 8 **C's** and 8 **reverse C's**. Repeat using navy **strip**.

11. Referring to Steps 5 and 6 of **Making the Pieced Border**, page 53, make 8 **Border Units**. (You will need 8 each of **Units 15 - 20**.)

12. Sew 2 **Border Units** together to make **Pieced Border**. Make 4 **Pieced Borders**.

Pieced Border (make 4)

13. Referring to **Wall Hanging Top Diagram**, sew 1 **Pieced Border** each to top and bottom edges of **Block**. Sew 1 **corner square** to each end of each remaining **Pieced Border**; sew borders to side edges of **Block** to make center section of wall hanging top.

14. Follow **Adding Squared Borders**, page 151, to sew **top**, **bottom**, then **side inner borders** to center section. Repeat to add **middle** and **outer borders** to complete **Wall Hanging Top**.

COMPLETING THE WALL HANGING

1. Follow **Quilting**, page 152, to mark, layer, and quilt using **Quilting Diagram**, page 54, as a suggestion. Our wall hanging is hand quilted.

2. Follow **Making a Hanging Sleeve**, page 156, to attach hanging sleeve to wall hanging back.

3. Follow **Binding**, page 154, to bind wall hanging using 2½"w straight-grain binding with overlapped corners.

Wall Hanging Top Diagram

CASTLE SQUARE SNUGGLE QUILT

SKILL LEVEL: 1 2 3 4 5
BLOCK SIZE: 9½" x 9½"
QUILT SIZE: 63" x 77"

YARDAGE REQUIREMENTS
Yardage is based on 45"w fabric.

■ 3¼ yds of light burgundy solid
■ 1⅛ yds of navy solid
■ 1 yd of burgundy solid
  4¾ yds for backing
  ⅞ yd for binding
  72" x 90" batting

CUTTING OUT THE PIECES
All measurements include a ¼" seam allowance. Follow Rotary Cutting, page 146, to cut fabric.

1. **From light burgundy solid:** ■
   • Cut 2 lengthwise **side borders** 5¼" x 81".
   • Cut 3 lengthwise **long sashing strips** 5¼" x 67".
   • Cut 2 lengthwise **top/bottom borders** 5¼" x 57".
   • Cut 4 strips 5¼"w. From these strips, cut 16 **short sashing strips** 5¼" x 10".

2. **From navy solid:**
   • Cut 6 strips 5⅝"w. From these strips, cut 40 squares 5⅝" x 5⅝". Cut squares once diagonally to make 80 **triangles**.
3. **From burgundy solid:**
   • Cut 4 strips 7¼"w. From these strips, cut 20 **squares** 7¼" x 7¼".

ASSEMBLING THE QUILT TOP

*Refer to photo, page 48, and follow **Piecing and Pressing**, page 148, to make quilt top.*

1. Sew 1 **square** and 4 **triangles** together to make **Block**. Make 20 **Blocks**.

Block (make 20)

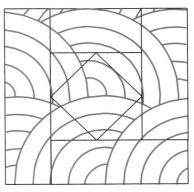

2. Sew 5 **Blocks** and 4 **short sashing strips** together to make vertical **Row**. Make 4 **Rows**.

Row (make 4)

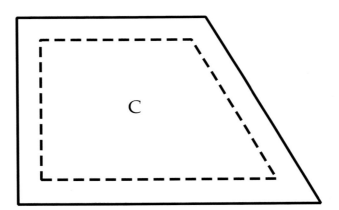

3. Sew **Rows** and **long sashing strips** together to make center section of quilt top.
4. Follow **Adding Squared Borders**, page 151, to add **top**, **bottom**, then **side borders** to center section to complete **Quilt Top**.

COMPLETING THE QUILT

1. Follow **Quilting**, page 152, to mark, layer, and quilt using **Quilting Diagram** as a suggestion. Our quilt is hand quilted.
2. Cut a 28" square of binding fabric. Follow **Binding**, page 154, to bind quilt using 2½"w bias binding with mitered corners.

Quilting Diagram

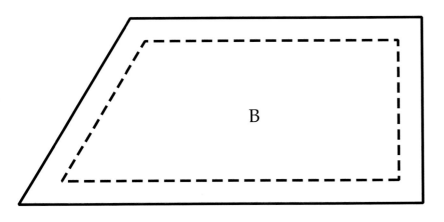

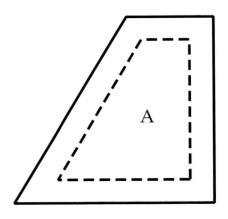

TRIP AROUND THE WORLD

Known *for their principles of separateness and plainness, the Amish are often recognized by the solemn cloaks that they wear for public outings. Those outside the religion seldom see the wonderfully vibrant shirts, aprons, dresses, and slips that illustrate the Amish affinity for color. That love is apparent in the Trip Around the World quilt pattern, a traditional Amish design that utilizes a spectrum of rich hues. For our version, we assembled the squares in rotary-cut, strip-pieced sets. We then simply stair-stepped the sets — similar to a bargello technique — to produce the quilt's diamond arrangement. The deep border provides a showcase for masterful quilting.*

TRIP AROUND THE WORLD QUILT

SKILL LEVEL: 1 **2** 3 4 5
QUILT SIZE: 96" x 114"

YARDAGE REQUIREMENTS

Yardage is based on 45"w fabric.

■ 5¹/₂ yds of navy solid

■ 3³/₈ yds of dark burgundy solid

◨ ¹/₂ yd *each* of rust, dark purple, teal, green, cream, dark burgundy, burgundy, pink, black, navy, light purple, brown, and purple solids
8³/₄ yds for backing
1 yd for binding
120" x 120" batting

CUTTING OUT THE PIECES

All measurements include a ¹/₄" seam allowance. Follow
Rotary Cutting, *page 146, to cut fabric.*

1. **From navy solid:** ■
   - Cut 2 lengthwise **top/bottom middle borders** 13" x 94".
   - Cut 2 lengthwise **side middle borders** 13" x 87".

2. **From dark burgundy solid:** ■
   - Cut 2 lengthwise **side outer borders** 2³/₄" x 112".
   - Cut 2 lengthwise **top/bottom outer borders** 2³/₄" x 99".
   - Cut 2 lengthwise **side inner borders** 2³/₄" x 83".
   - Cut 2 lengthwise **top/bottom inner borders** 2³/₄" x 69".

3. **From rust, dark purple, teal, green, cream, dark burgundy, burgundy, pink, black, navy, light purple, brown, and purple solids:** ◨
   - Cut 5 strips 2³/₄"w from *each* fabric.

ASSEMBLING THE QUILT TOP

Follow **Piecing and Pressing**, *page 148, to make quilt top.*

1. Sew 1 **strip** of each color together in color order shown to make **Strip Set**. Make 5 **Strip Sets**.

Strip Set (make 5)

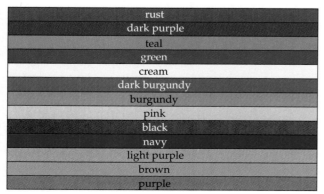

rust
dark purple
teal
green
cream
dark burgundy
burgundy
pink
black
navy
light purple
brown
purple

2. With right sides together and matching long raw edges, sew final lengthwise seam of 1 **Strip Set** to form a tube (**Fig. 1**). Repeat with remaining **Strip Sets**.

Fig. 1

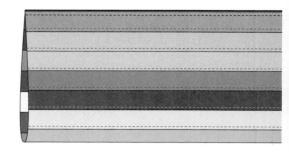

3. Referring to **Fig. 2**, cut across **Strip Sets** at 2³/₄" intervals to make 75 circular **Strip Units**.

Fig. 2

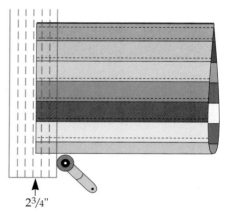

2³/₄"

Strip Unit (make 75)

4. Refer to **Quarter Section** diagrams to determine which color square to place at the top of each **Strip Unit**. Use a seam ripper to remove seam above determined top square of each **Strip Unit** (**Fig. 3**). Working from left to right on a flat surface, carefully arrange **Strip Units** in correct order. Sew **Strip Units** together to make 2 **Quarter Section A's** and 2 **Quarter Section B's**.

Fig. 3

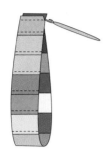

Quarter Section A (make 2)

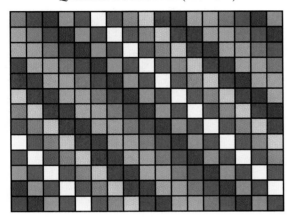

Quarter Section B (make 2)

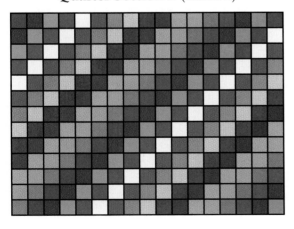

5. Remove seam above purple square of 1 **Strip Unit** to make **Unit 1**. Make 4 **Unit 1's**.

Unit 1 (make 4)

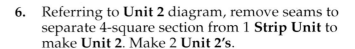

6. Referring to **Unit 2** diagram, remove seams to separate 4-square section from 1 **Strip Unit** to make **Unit 2**. Make 2 **Unit 2's**.

Unit 2 (make 2)

7. Sew 1 **Unit 1** and 1 **Unit 2** together to make **Unit 3**. Make 2 **Unit 3's**.

Unit 3 (make 2)

8. Remove seams to separate 1 brown square from 1 **Strip Unit** to make **center square**.

center square

9. Referring to **Assembly Diagram**, page 62, sew **Quarter Section A's**, **Quarter Section B's**, **Unit 1's**, **Unit 3's**, and **center square** together to make center section of quilt top.
10. Follow **Adding Squared Borders**, page 151, to add **side**, then **top** and **bottom inner borders** to center section. Repeat to add **middle** and **outer borders** to complete **Quilt Top**.

COMPLETING THE QUILT
1. Follow **Quilting**, page 152, to mark, layer, and quilt using **Quilting Diagram** as a suggestion. Our quilt is hand quilted.
2. Cut a 32" square of binding fabric. Follow **Binding**, page 154, to bind quilt using 2¹/₂"w bias binding with mitered corners.

Quilting Diagram

Assembly Diagram

Quarter Section A Unit 3 **Quarter Section B**

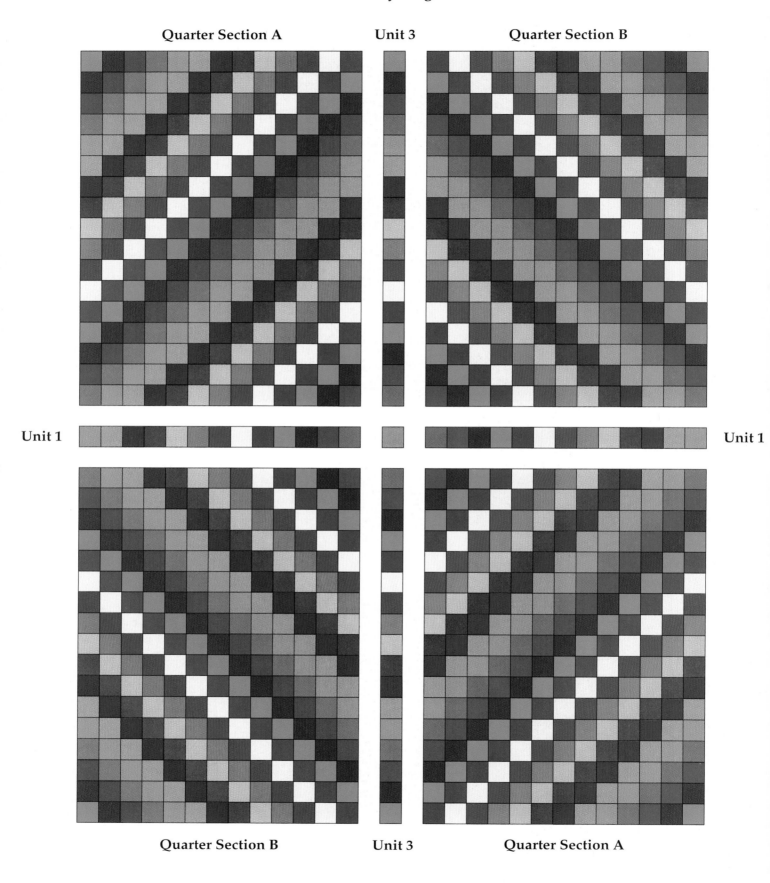

Unit 1

Unit 1

Quarter Section B Unit 3 **Quarter Section A**

PANSY COLLECTION

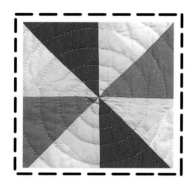

Tender heart-shaped leaves and blossoms that resemble cheery faces have made the pansy one of the most endearing garden favorites. Their vivid blooms (symbols of thoughtfulness in the language of flowers) brighten chilly days with delightful shades of purple, blue, and yellow. Reflecting those vibrant hues, this bright quilt unites two variations of the traditional Pinwheel block — one created with easy triangle-squares, the other a sunny combination of basic triangles. Setting the blocks together without sashing produces a captivating kaleidoscope of colors. Finished with a series of plain borders, the quilt is enhanced by a bouquet of coordinating accessories that feature the thoughtful pansy.

Abloom with royal hues, these lovely accents will brighten any room with femininity. Nosegays of pretty pansies are appliquéd onto a charming wall hanging (opposite) *and matching throw pillow* (left). *The blossoms also look lovely when added to an elegant valance and curtain tiebacks* (below).

PINWHEEL QUILT

SKILL LEVEL: 1 2 3 4 5
BLOCK SIZE: 8" x 8"
QUILT SIZE: 83" x 99"

YARDAGE REQUIREMENTS

Yardage is based on 45" wide fabric.

- 3 3/8 yds of purple solid
- 3 3/8 yds of yellow solid
- 3 1/4 yds of white solid
- 2 7/8 yds of blue solid
- 7/8 yd of light purple solid
- 7 5/8 yds for backing
- 1 yd for binding
- 90" x 108" batting

CUTTING OUT THE PIECES

All measurements include a 1/4" seam allowance. Follow ***Rotary Cutting****, page 146, to cut fabric.*

1. **From purple solid:**
   - Cut 5 strips 4 7/8"w. From these strips, cut 40 squares 4 7/8" x 4 7/8". Cut squares once diagonally to make 80 **large triangles**.
   - Cut 2 lengthwise **side middle borders** 2 3/4" x 87".
   - Cut 2 lengthwise **top/bottom middle borders** 2 3/4" x 76".
   - Cut 7 **rectangles** 11" x 16" for triangle-squares.
2. **From yellow solid:**
   - Cut 5 strips 5 1/4"w. From these strips, cut 40 squares 5 1/4" x 5 1/4". Cut squares twice diagonally to make 160 **small triangles**.
   - Cut 2 lengthwise **side inner borders** 2" x 84".
   - Cut 2 lengthwise **top/bottom inner borders** 2" x 71".
3. **From white solid:**
   - Cut 7 strips 11"w. From these strips, cut 14 **rectangles** 11" x 16" for triangle-squares.
   - Cut 5 strips 5 1/4"w. From these strips, cut 40 squares 5 1/4" x 5 1/4". Cut squares twice diagonally to make 160 **small triangles**.
4. **From blue solid:**
   - Cut 2 lengthwise **side outer borders** 5 1/2" x 92".
   - Cut 2 lengthwise **top/bottom outer borders** 5 1/2" x 86".
   - Cut 7 **rectangles** 11" x 16" for triangle-squares.
5. **From light purple solid:**
   - Cut 5 strips 4 7/8"w. From these strips, cut 40 squares 4 7/8" x 4 7/8". Cut squares once diagonally to make 80 **large triangles**.

ASSEMBLING THE QUILT TOP

Follow ***Piecing and Pressing****, page 148, to make quilt top.*

1. To make triangle-squares, place 1 white and 1 purple **rectangle** right sides together. Referring to **Fig. 1**, follow **Making Triangle-Squares**, page 148, to make 12 **purple triangle-squares**. Repeat with remaining **rectangles** to make a total of 84 **purple triangle-squares** and 84 **blue triangle-squares**. (From each color combination, you will need 80 and have 4 left over.)

Fig. 1

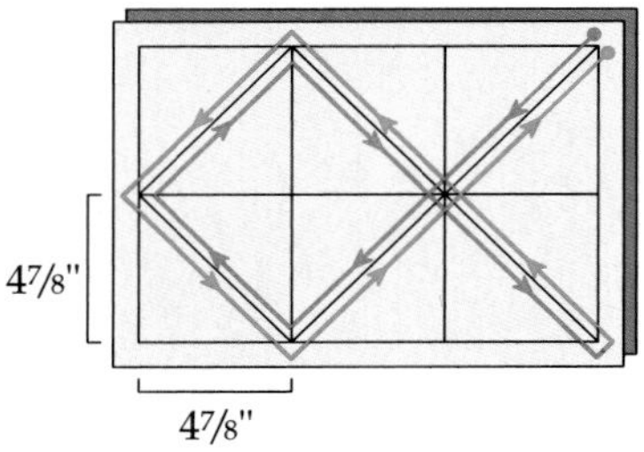

purple triangle-square (make 84)

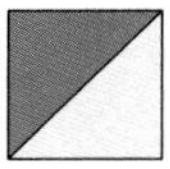

blue triangle-square (make 84)

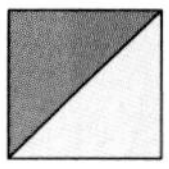

2. Sew 4 **triangle-squares** together to make **Block A**. Make 40 **Block A's**.

Block A (make 40)

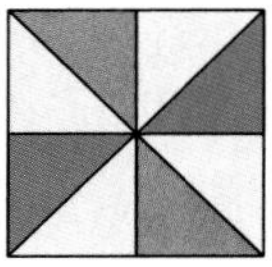

3. Sew 2 **small triangles** together to make **Unit 1**. Make 160 **Unit 1's**.

Unit 1 (make 160)

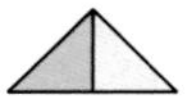

4. Sew 1 **Unit 1** and 1 **large triangle** together to make **Unit 2**. Make 80 **Unit 2's**.

Unit 2 (make 80)

5. Sew 1 **Unit 1** and 1 **large triangle** together to make **Unit 3**. Make 80 **Unit 3's**.

Unit 3 (make 80)

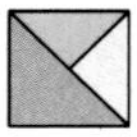

6. Sew 2 **Unit 2's** and 2 **Unit 3's** together to make **Block B**. Make 40 **Block B's**.

Block B (make 40)

7. Referring to **Quilt Top Diagram**, sew 4 **Block A's** and 4 **Block B's** together to make **Row**. Make 10 **Rows**.

Row (make 10)

8. Referring to **Quilt Top Diagram**, sew **Rows** together to make center section of quilt top.
9. Follow **Adding Squared Borders**, page 151, to sew **side**, then **top** and **bottom inner borders** to center section. Repeat to add **middle** and **outer borders** to complete **Quilt Top**.

Quilt Top Diagram

COMPLETING THE QUILT

1. Follow **Quilting**, page 152, to mark, layer, and quilt using **Quilting Diagram** as a suggestion. Our quilt is hand quilted.
2. Cut a 32" square of binding fabric. Follow **Binding**, page 154, to bind quilt using 2¹/₂"w bias binding with mitered corners.

Quilting Diagram

PANSY WALL HANGING

SKILL LEVEL: 1 2 3 4 5
BLOCK SIZE: 11" x 11"
WALL HANGING SIZE: 31" x 44"

YARDAGE REQUIREMENTS

Yardage is based on 45"w fabric.

- 1¹/₂ yds of blue solid
- ³/₄ yd of white solid
- ¹/₂ yd of dark green solid
- 1 fat quarter (18" x 22" piece) *each* of light green, very light purple, light purple, purple, dark purple, navy, light yellow, yellow, and dark yellow
  1¹/₂ yds for backing and hanging sleeve
  ¹/₂ yd for binding
  34" x 48" batting

You will also need:
  template plastic
  ¹/₄"w bias pressing bar
  purple embroidery floss

CUTTING OUT THE PIECES

All measurements include a ¹/₄" seam allowance. Follow Rotary Cutting, page 146, to cut fabric.

1. **From blue solid:**
   - Cut 2 lengthwise **side borders** 3" x 47".
   - Cut 1 **long sashing strip** 3" x 38¹/₂".
   - Cut 2 **top/bottom borders** 3" x 34".
   - Cut 4 **short sashing strips** 3" x 11¹/₂".

2. **From white solid:**
   - Cut 2 strips 11¹/₂"w. From these strips, cut 6 **background squares** 11¹/₂" x 11¹/₂".

3. **From dark green solid:**
   - Cut 1 **square** 16" x 16" for bias strip.

ASSEMBLING THE WALL HANGING TOP

Follow Piecing and Pressing, page 148, to make wall hanging top.

1. Use patterns, page 74, and follow Step 1 of **Template Cutting**, page 147, to make 1 template *each* of patterns **A - L**.
2. Using **Block** diagram, page 71, as a suggestion for fabric colors, refer to **Hand Appliqué**, page 151, to make appliqués. For *each* **Block**, you will need:

4 **A's**	3 **G's**
4 **B's**	2 **H's**
4 **C's**	2 **I's**
3 **D's** (1 in reverse)	1 **J**
3 **E's** (1 in reverse)	2 **K's** (1 in reverse)
3 **F's** (1 in reverse)	2 **L's** (1 in reverse)

3. To make bias tube for stems, use **square** and follow Steps 1 - 6 of **Making Continuous Bias Strip Binding**, page 154, to make 1"w continuous bias strip.
4. Fold bias strip in half lengthwise with wrong sides together; do not press. Stitch ¹/₄" from long raw edge to form tube; trim seam allowance to ¹/₈". Place bias pressing bar inside 1 end of tube. Center seam at back of bar and press as you move bar down length of tube. Cut tube to desired lengths for stems.
5. Following **Block** diagram to layer and arrange appliqués and stem pieces on **background square**, refer to **Hand Appliqué**, page 151, to stitch appliqués to background square to complete **Block**. Make 6 **Blocks**.
6. On *each* **Block**, use 3 strands of embroidery floss and **Satin Stitch**, page 158, to work a ¹/₄" circle in the center of each open pansy.

Block (make 6)

6. Sew 3 **Blocks** and 2 **short sashing strips** together to make vertical **Row**. Make 2 **Rows**.

Row (make 2)

7. Sew **Rows** and **long sashing strip** together to make center section of wall hanging.
8. Referring to **Wall Hanging Top Diagram**, follow **Adding Mitered Borders**, page 151, to add **borders** to complete **Wall Hanging Top**.

COMPLETING THE WALL HANGING

1. Follow **Quilting**, page 152, to mark, layer, and quilt wall hanging using **Quilting Diagram** as a suggestion. Our wall hanging is hand quilted.
2. Follow **Making a Hanging Sleeve**, page 156, to attach hanging sleeve to wall hanging.
3. Follow **Binding**, page 154, to bind wall hanging using 1½"w bias binding with mitered corners.

Wall Hanging Top Diagram

Quilting Diagram

BOUQUET PILLOW

PILLOW SIZE: 16" x 16"

SUPPLIES

11½" x 11½" **background square** of white solid fabric

4 strips 3" x 17" of blue solid fabric for **borders**

18" x 18" square of fabric for pillow top backing

18" x 18" square of fabric for pillow back

scraps of assorted fabrics for appliqués

28" of 1"w bias fabric strip for stems

2 yds of 2"w bias fabric strip for welting

2 yds of ¼" cord for welting

template plastic

¼"w bias pressing bar

purple embroidery floss

polyester fiberfill

MAKING THE PILLOW

*Refer to photo and follow **Piecing and Pressing**, page 148, to make pillow.*

1. Follow Steps 1 and 2 of **Assembling the Wall Hanging Top**, page 70, to make appliqués for 1 **Block**.
2. Use 1"w bias strip and refer to Steps 4 and 5 of **Assembling the Wall Hanging Top**, page 70, to make bias tube for stems and to complete 1 **Block**.
3. Follow **Adding Mitered Borders**, page 151, to sew **borders** to **Block** to complete **Pillow Top**.
4. Use 3 strands of embroidery floss and **Satin Stitch**, page 158, to work a ¼" circle in the center of each open pansy.
5. Follow **Quilting**, page 152, to mark, layer, and quilt pillow top. Our pillow top is hand quilted in the ditch around appliqués and at ½" intervals outside appliquéd motif.
6. Follow **Pillow Finishing**, page 157, to complete pillow with welting.

Pillow Top Diagram

PANSY VALANCE

VALANCE SIZE: 13" x 36"

Our valance will fit a window approximately 28" to 30" wide.

SUPPLIES

2 **rectangles** 17" x 42" of white solid fabric for valance top and valance backing

scraps of light green, dark green, light purple, purple, dark purple, light blue, blue, dark blue, yellow, and white solid fabrics for appliqués

40" of 1"w bias fabric strip for vine

1½ yds of 1½"w bias fabric strip for binding

15" x 38" batting

template plastic

¼"w bias pressing bar

purple and green embroidery floss

MAKING THE VALANCE

*Follow **Piecing and Pressing**, page 148, to make valance.*

1. Use patterns, page 75, and follow **Template Cutting**, page 147, to make 1 template *each* of patterns **M - Z** and **AA - MM**.
2. Using **Valance Diagram**, page 71, as a suggestion for fabric colors, refer to **Hand Appliqué**, page 151, to make appliqués for valance. You will need:
   1 *each* of **N**, **Q**, **S**, and **T**
   2 *each* (1 in reverse) of **M**, **O**, **P**, **R**, **U - Z**
   2 *each* (1 in reverse) of **BB - MM**
   6 (3 in reverse) of **AA**
3. Use 1"w bias fabric strip and follow Step 4 of **Assembling the Wall Hanging**, page 70, to make bias tube for vines.
4. Following **Valance Diagram** to layer and arrange appliqués and vine pieces on valance top, refer to **Hand Appliqué**, page 151, to stitch appliqués to valance top.
5. Referring to **Valance Diagram**, use 2 strands of embroidery floss and **Stem Stitch**, page 158, to add details to appliqués.
6. Trim valance top to measure 16" x 40". Follow **Quilting**, page 152, to mark, layer, and quilt valance top. Our valance is hand quilted in a 1" grid design. Trim batting and backing even with valance top.
7. Press ends of valance 1" to wrong side. Press under 1" again; blindstitch folded edge to backing.
8. To make rod pocket, press top raw edge of valance 1" to wrong side. Press 2" to wrong side again; blindstitch folded edge to backing.
9. To mark scallops on lower edge of valance, begin 3" from left side of valance and space dots 6" apart, marking dots 1" from bottom edge (**Fig. 1**). Use a compass or round object to draw scalloped lines connecting dots. Do not trim.

Fig. 1

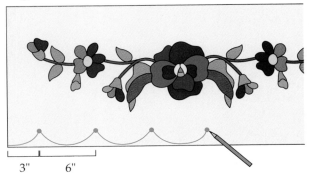

3" 6"

10. Matching wrong sides and raw edges, fold bias fabric strip in half lengthwise to make binding.

11. Matching raw edges of binding to scalloped line and leaving an extra 1/2" of binding at each end, follow Steps 1 and 2 of **Attaching Binding with Mitered Corners**, page 156, to pin binding to front lower edge of valance. Using a 1/4" seam allowance and easing around curves, sew binding to valance. Trim valance top, batting, and backing even with edge of binding. Fold each end of binding over to valance back and pin in place. Fold binding over to valance back covering stitching line; blindstitch in place.

Valance Diagram

PANSY CURTAIN TIEBACKS

TIEBACK SIZE: 3¹/₂" x 17"

Instructions are for making 1 pair of tiebacks.

SUPPLIES
4 rectangles 4" x 17¹/₂" white solid fabric for **tieback tops** and **tieback backings**
scraps of green, light green, blue, and dark blue solid fabrics for appliqués
12" of 1"w bias fabric strip for stems
2¹/₂ yds of 1¹/₂"w bias fabric strip for binding
2 rectangles 4" x 17¹/₂" of batting
template plastic
¹/₄"w bias pressing bar
4 small cabone (drapery) rings

MAKING THE TIEBACKS
*Follow **Piecing and Pressing**, page 148, to make tiebacks.*

1. Use patterns, page 75, and follow **Template Cutting**, page 147, to make 1 template *each* of patterns **KK - NN**.

2. Using **Tieback Diagram** as a suggestion for fabric colors, refer to **Hand Appliqué**, page 151, to make appliqués for valance. You will need:
   2 **KK's** (1 in reverse)
   2 **LL's** (1 in reverse)
   2 **MM's** (1 in reverse)
   4 **NN's** (2 in reverse)

3. Use 1"w bias fabric strip and follow Step 4 of **Assembling the Wall Hanging Top**, page 70, to make bias tube for stems.

4. Following **Tieback Diagram** to layer and arrange appliqués and stems on each tieback top, refer to **Hand Appliqué**, page 151, to stitch appliqués to tieback tops.

5. Follow **Quilting**, page 152, to layer and quilt. Our tiebacks are hand quilted in the ditch around each appliqué.

6. Use a compass or round object to draw a rounded end on each end of each tieback. Trim on drawn line.

7. Matching wrong sides and raw edges, fold 1¹/₂"w bias fabric strip in half lengthwise to make binding. Matching raw edges and easing around curves, pin binding to front of each tieback. Trim excess binding 1" past overlap. Press top end ¹/₂" to wrong side. Using a ¹/₄" seam allowance, sew binding to tieback. Fold binding over to back of each tieback and pin in place, covering stitching line. Blindstitch binding to tieback backings.

8. Sew 1 ring to backing at each end of each tieback.

Tieback Diagram

LOG CABIN LULLABY

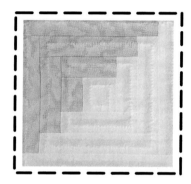

Snuggled under this precious Log Cabin quilt, baby will be wrapped in all the love and warmth that the timeless pattern brings to mind. For our cozy coverlet, we built each block around a white center square — a symbol for the tender innocence of a newborn. As each fabric strip is added, it's quickly and easily trimmed to the exact size you need, so you don't have to worry with tiny pieces. The pretty pastels used in the blocks are accented by pink corner squares and rainbow-look binding. Completed with sweet quilting motifs, this soft, cuddly quilt will be a fitting gift from the heart.

LOG CABIN LULLABY CRIB QUILT

SKILL LEVEL: 1 2 3 4 5
BLOCK SIZE: 5³⁄₄" x 5³⁄₄"
QUILT SIZE: 38" x 50"

YARDAGE REQUIREMENTS
Yardage is based on 45"w fabric.

- ☐ 1¹⁄₂ yds of white solid
- ▨ ¹⁄₂ yd of pink check
- ▨ ¹⁄₄ yd of pink print
- ◹ ¹⁄₄ yd *each* of yellow print, yellow check, blue print, blue stripe, blue check, purple print, purple check, green print, green stripe, and aqua print
  2³⁄₄ yds for backing
  45" x 60" batting

CUTTING OUT THE PIECES
All measurements include a ¹⁄₄" seam allowance. Follow
Rotary Cutting, *page 146, to cut fabric.*

1. **From white solid:** ☐
   - Cut 1 strip 1³⁄₄"w. From this strip, cut 24 **squares** 1³⁄₄" x 1³⁄₄".
   - Cut 18 **strips** 1¹⁄₄"w.
   - Cut 2 **side outer borders** 5¹⁄₂" x 39".
   - Cut 2 **top/bottom outer borders** 5¹⁄₂" x 27¹⁄₂".

2. **From pink check:** ▨
   - Cut 2 **side inner borders** 2¹⁄₂" x 39".
   - Cut 2 **top/bottom inner borders** 2¹⁄₂" x 23¹⁄₂".
   - Cut 2 **strips** 1¹⁄₄"w.

3. **From pink print:** ▨
   - Cut 1 strip 5¹⁄₂"w. From this strip, cut 4 **corner squares** 5¹⁄₂" x 5¹⁄₂".
   - Cut 2 **strips** 1¹⁄₄"w.

4. **From yellow print, yellow check, blue print, blue stripe, blue check, purple print, purple check, green print, green stripe, and aqua print:** ◹
   - Cut 2 **strips** 1¹⁄₄"w from *each* fabric.

ASSEMBLING THE QUILT TOP
Follow **Piecing and Pressing**, *page 148, to make quilt top.*

1. Place 1 pink check **strip** on 1 **square** with right sides together and raw edges matching. Stitch as shown in **Fig. 1**. Trim **strip** even with **square** (**Fig. 2**); press open (**Fig. 3**).

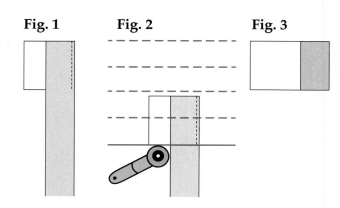

Fig. 1   **Fig. 2**   **Fig. 3**

2. Turn **square** ¹⁄₄ turn to the left and repeat Step 1 to add the next "log" as shown in **Figs. 4 - 6**.

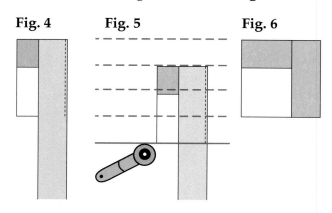

Fig. 4   **Fig. 5**   **Fig. 6**

3. Repeat Step 2 to add white **strips** to remaining 2 sides of **square** (**Fig. 7**).

Fig. 7

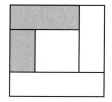

4. Continue adding **strips**, alternating 2 pink check strips and 2 white strips until there are 3 strips on each side of square to make **Block**. Make 2 **Blocks** using pink check and white strips.

Block

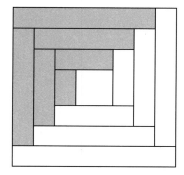

5. Using remaining strips, repeat Steps 1 - 4 to make a total of 24 **Blocks** (2 Blocks using *each* color print, check, or stripe).
6. Referring to **Quilt Top Diagram** for color placement, sew **Blocks** together into rows. Sew rows together to make center section of quilt top.
7. Sew **top**, **bottom**, then **side inner borders** to center section.
8. Sew 1 **corner square** to each end of each **side outer border**. Sew **top**, **bottom**, then **side outer borders** to center section to complete **Quilt Top**.

COMPLETING THE QUILT

1. Follow **Quilting**, page 152, to mark, layer, and quilt using **Quilting Diagram** as a suggestion. Our quilt is hand quilted.
2. To make pieced binding, cut remaining scraps of print, check, and stripe fabrics into pieces 2¹/₂"w and varying in length from 3¹/₂" to 6¹/₂". Sew pieces together along 2¹/₂"w edges to make 2 **top/bottom binding pieces** 40"l and 2 **side binding pieces** 52"l. Follow **Attaching Binding with Overlapped Corners**, page 156, to bind quilt.

Quilting Diagram

Quilt Top Diagram

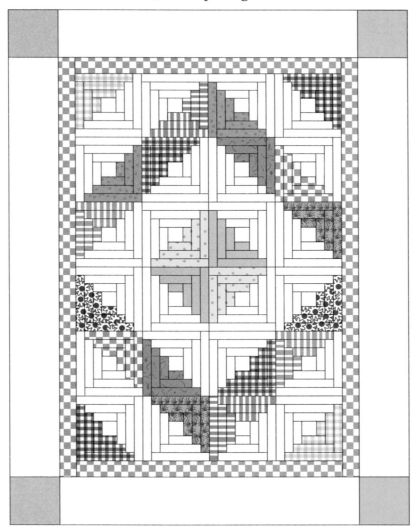

79

AMISH COLLECTION

As Amish congregations moved into the Midwest during the late 1800's, many rules for daily living were established by the leaders in each community. Church districts soon developed their own unique customs, especially those regarding quilt patterns and colors. The Crosses and Losses quilt shown here is typical of the designs made by Amish quilters in Ohio. The seamstresses often used black as a main background color and alternated pieced blocks with plain squares. Our version of the simple pattern is made with an easy grid method for the triangle-squares. Complemented by a red inner border, the quilt has ample areas for beautiful feather wreath and cable quilting.

*T*he pattern of this sweet wall hanging (opposite) is named for shoofly pie, a traditional Amish dessert made with butter, molasses, and brown sugar. Each Shoofly block uses grid-pieced units in shades of blue, green, red, or purple, creating a tone-on-tone effect. Vivid jewel tones are also used to create an Amish version of our Log Cabin crib quilt (below). This versatile design can be displayed as a unique wall hanging or a tabletop accent, too. Instructions for making the Log Cabin project begin on page 78.

CROSSES AND LOSSES QUILT

SKILL LEVEL: 1 2 3 4 5
BLOCK SIZE: 9" x 9"
QUILT SIZE: 95" x 108"

Because of the quick methods used to duplicate the scrappy look of our quilt, you will have some pieces left over after assembling the blocks.

YARDAGE REQUIREMENTS
Yardage is based on 45" wide fabric.

- 7¹/₂ yds of black solid
- 2⁷/₈ yds of dark red solid
- 1 fat quarter (18" x 22" piece) *each* of 11 assorted solids
  8³/₈ yds for backing
  1¹/₈ yds for binding
  120" x 120" batting

CUTTING OUT THE PIECES
All measurements include a ¹/₄" seam allowance. Follow ***Rotary Cutting***, *page 146, to cut fabric.*

1. **From black solid:**
   - Cut 4 strips 11"w. From these strips, cut 11 **rectangles** 11" x 14" for triangle-squares.
   - Cut 12 strips 2³/₄"w. From these strips, cut 168 **squares** 2³/₄" x 2³/₄".
   - Cut 7 strips 3¹/₈"w. From these strips, cut 84 squares 3¹/₈" x 3¹/₈". Cut squares once diagonally to make 168 **small triangles**.
   - Cut 8 strips 9¹/₂"w. From these strips, cut 30 **setting squares** 9¹/₂" x 9¹/₂".
   - Cut 4 lengthwise **outer borders** 7" x 98".
   - From remaining fabric width, cut 6 squares 14" x 14". Cut squares twice diagonally to make 24 **side triangles**. (You will need 22 and have 2 left over.)
   - From remaining fabric width, cut 2 squares 7¹/₄" x 7¹/₄". Cut squares once diagonally to make 4 **corner triangles**.

2. **From dark red solid:**
   - Cut 2 lengthwise **inner side borders** 2³/₄" x 94".
   - Cut 2 lengthwise **inner top/bottom borders** 2³/₄" x 85".

3. **From *each* of 11 assorted solids:**
   - Cut 1 **rectangle** 11" x 14" for triangle-squares.
   - Cut 4 squares 5³/₈" x 5³/₈". Cut squares once diagonally to make 8 **large triangles**.

ASSEMBLING THE QUILT TOP
*Follow **Piecing and Pressing**, page 148, to make quilt top.*

1. To make triangle-squares, place 1 solid and 1 black **rectangle** right sides together. Referring to **Fig. 1**, follow **Making Triangle-Squares**, page 148, to make 24 **triangle-squares**.

Fig. 1

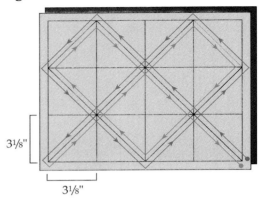

3¹/₈"

3¹/₈"

triangle-square (make 24)

2. Sew 2 **triangle-squares** and 2 **squares** together to make **Unit 1**. Make 8 **Unit 1's**.

Unit 1 (make 8)

3. Sew 1 **triangle-square** and 2 **small triangles** together to make **Unit 2**. Make 8 **Unit 2's**.

Unit 2 (make 8)

4. Sew 1 **large triangle** and 1 **Unit 2** together to make **Unit 3**. Make 8 **Unit 3's**.

Unit 3 (make 8)

5. Sew 2 **Unit 3's** and 2 **Unit 1's** together to make **Block**. Make 4 **Blocks**.

Block (make 4)

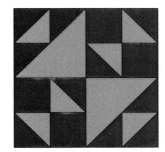

6. Repeat Steps 1 - 5 to make a total of 42 **Blocks**.
7. Referring to **Assembly Diagram**, page 86, sew **corner triangles**, **side triangles**, **Blocks**, and **setting squares** together into diagonal rows. Sew rows together to make center section of quilt top.
8. Follow **Adding Squared Borders**, page 151, to sew **side**, then **top** and **bottom inner borders** to center section. Repeat to add **outer borders** to complete **Quilt Top**.

COMPLETING THE QUILT

1. Follow **Quilting**, page 152, to mark, layer, and quilt using **Quilting Diagram** as a suggestion. Our quilt is hand quilted.

2. Cut a 34" square of binding fabric. Follow **Binding**, page 154, to bind quilt using 2¹/₂"w bias binding with mitered corners.

Quilting Diagram

Quilt Top Diagram

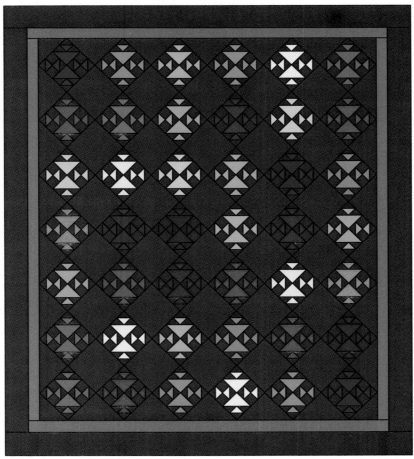

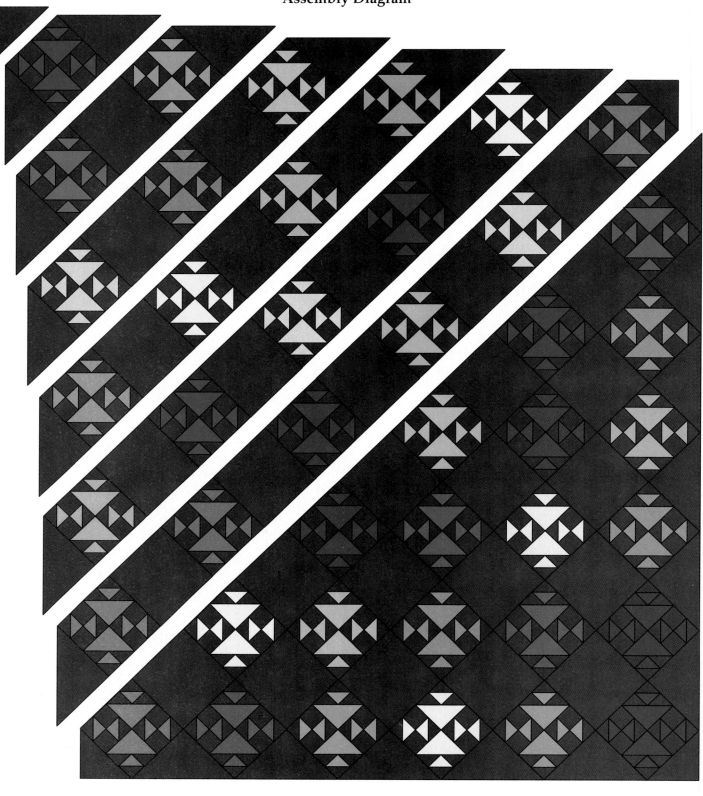

SHOOFLY WALL HANGING

SKILL LEVEL: 1 2 3 4 5
BLOCK SIZE: 4⁷/₈" x 4⁷/₈"
WALL HANGING SIZE: 35" x 42"

YARDAGE REQUIREMENTS

Yardage is based on 45"w fabric.

- 1¹/₈ yds of black solid
- ³/₈ yd of dark red solid
- ¹/₄ yd of purple solid
- scraps of assorted medium solids
- scraps of assorted dark solids
  1³/₈ yds for backing and hanging sleeve
  ³/₄ yd for binding
  38" x 45" batting

CUTTING OUT THE PIECES

All measurements include a ¹/₄" seam allowance. Follow
Rotary Cutting*, page 146, to cut fabric.*

1. **From black solid:**
   - Cut 2 **side outer borders** 5" x 32³/₈".
   - Cut 2 **top/bottom outer borders** 5" x 25³/₈".
   - Cut 3 squares 8¹/₄" x 8¹/₄". Cut squares twice diagonally to make 12 **side triangles**. (You will need 10 and have 2 left over.)
   - Cut 6 **setting squares** 5³/₈" x 5³/₈".
   - Cut 2 squares 4³/₈" x 4³/₈". Cut squares once diagonally to make 4 **corner triangles**.

2. **From dark red solid:**
   - Cut 2 **side inner borders** 2⁵/₈" x 32³/₈".
   - Cut 2 **top/bottom inner borders** 2⁵/₈" x 21¹/₈".

3. **From purple solid:**
   - Cut 4 **corner squares** 5" x 5".

4. **From assorted medium solids:**
   - For *each* of 12 blocks, cut 1 **rectangle** 4" x 6¹/₂" for triangle-squares and 4 **squares** 2¹/₈" x 2¹/₈".

5. **From assorted dark solids:**
   - For *each* of 12 blocks, cut 1 **rectangle** 4" x 6¹/₂" for triangle-squares and 1 **square** 2¹/₈" x 2¹/₈".

ASSEMBLING THE WALL HANGING TOP

*Follow **Piecing and Pressing**, page 148, to make wall hanging top.*

1. To make triangle-squares, place 1 medium solid and 1 dark solid **rectangle** right sides together. Referring to **Fig. 1**, follow **Making Triangle-Squares**, page 148, to make 4 **triangle-squares**.

Fig. 1

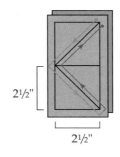

2½"

2½"

triangle-square (make 4)

2. Sew 2 **triangle-squares** and 1 **square** together to make **Unit 1**. Make 2 **Unit 1's**.

Unit 1 (make 2)

3. Sew 3 **squares** together to make 1 **Unit 2**.

Unit 2 (make 1)

4. Sew **Unit 1's** and **Unit 2** together to make **Block**.

Block

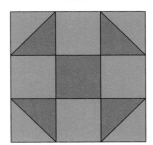

5. Repeat Steps 1 - 4 to make a total of 12 **Blocks**.
6. Referring to **Assembly Diagram**, sew **corner triangles**, **side triangles**, **Blocks**, and **setting squares** together into diagonal rows. Sew rows together to make center section of wall hanging top.
7. Sew **top**, **bottom**, then **side inner borders** to center section.
8. Sew **top** and **bottom outer borders** to center section. Sew 1 **corner square** to each end of **side outer borders**; sew **borders** to center section to complete **Wall Hanging Top**.

COMPLETING THE WALL HANGING

1. Follow **Quilting**, page 152, to mark, layer, and quilt using **Quilting Diagram** as a suggestion. Our wall hanging is hand quilted.
2. Follow **Making a Hanging Sleeve**, page 156, to attach hanging sleeve to wall hanging.
3. Cut a 22" square of binding fabric. Follow **Binding**, page 154, to bind wall hanging using 2¹⁄₂"w bias binding with overlapped corners.

Assembly Diagram

Wall Hanging Top Diagram

Quilting Diagram

CALICO COURTHOUSE STEPS

One beloved fabric defined the look of American fashions in the mid-1800's: the calico print. Its popularity soared as industrial advances — such as improved colorfast dyes and the expansion of railroad service — made the fabric widely available. Stitchers snapped up the calicoes for doing handiwork, especially their favorite quilting design, the Log Cabin pattern. A procession of many-colored calicoes, our charming quilt is set in a Log Cabin arrangement known as Courthouse Steps. The blocks begin with center units that are quickly cut from strip-pieced sets. As each "log" is added, it's simply trimmed to the size you need. The quilt is edged with a floral stripe print, which gives the illusion of many intricate borders in one easy step!

COURTHOUSE STEPS QUILT

SKILL LEVEL: 1 2 3 4 5
BLOCK SIZE: 9" x 9"
QUILT SIZE: 68" x 77"

YARDAGE REQUIREMENTS
Yardage is based on 45"w fabric.

- 4 yds of assorted dark prints
- 3 yds of assorted light prints
- 2½ yds of floral stripe print for border
- ¼ yd of pink print
- ⅛ yd of green print
  4¾ yds for backing
  1 yd for binding
  81" x 96" batting

CUTTING OUT THE PIECES
All measurements include a ¼" seam allowance. Follow
Rotary Cutting*, page 146, to cut fabric.*

1. **From assorted dark prints:**
   - Cut 80 **strips** 1½"w.
2. **From assorted light prints:**
   - Cut 60 **strips** 1½"w.
3. **From floral stripe for border:**
   - Cut 2 lengthwise **side borders** 2½" x 80".
   - Cut 2 lengthwise **top/bottom borders** 2½" x 71".
4. **From pink print:**
   - Cut 4 **strips** 1½"w.
5. **From green print:**
   - Cut 2 **strips** 1½"w.

ASSEMBLING THE QUILT TOP
*Follow **Piecing and Pressing**, page 148, to make quilt top.*

1. Sew 1 green and 2 pink print **strips** together to make **Strip Set**. Make 2 **Strip Sets**. Cut across **Strip Sets** at 1½" intervals to make 56 **Unit 1's**.

Strip Set (make 2)   **Unit 1** (make 56)

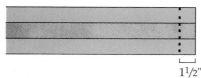

1½"

2. Place 1 dark print **strip** on 1 **Unit 1** with right sides together and matching 1 long raw edge of **strip** with long raw edge of **Unit 1**. Stitch as shown in **Fig. 1**. Trim **strip** even with **Unit 1** (**Fig. 2**); open and press (**Fig. 3**).

Fig. 1   **Fig. 2**   **Fig. 3**

 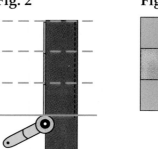 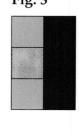

3. Repeat Step 2 to add matching dark print **strip** to opposite edge of **Unit 1** to make **Unit 2**.

Unit 2

4. Repeat Step 2 to add 2 matching light print **strips** to remaining edges of **Unit 2** to make **Unit 3**.

Unit 3

5. Continue to add **strips**, alternating 2 matching dark and 2 matching light print **strips**, until there are 4 **strips** on each side of center square to complete **Block**.

Block

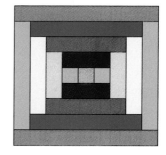

6. Repeat Steps 2 - 5 to make 56 **Blocks**.
7. Sew 7 **Blocks** together to make **Row**. Make 8 **Rows**.

Row (make 8)

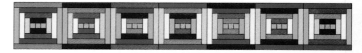

8. Referring to **Quilt Top Diagram**, sew **Rows** together to make center section of quilt top.
9. Follow **Adding Mitered Borders**, page 151, to sew borders to center section to complete **Quilt Top**.

COMPLETING THE QUILT

1. Follow **Quilting**, page 152, to mark, layer, and quilt. Our quilt is hand quilted using a diagonal grid pattern.
2. Cut a 30" square of binding fabric. Follow **Binding**, page 154, to bind quilt using 2¹/₂"w bias binding with mitered corners.

Quilt Top Diagram

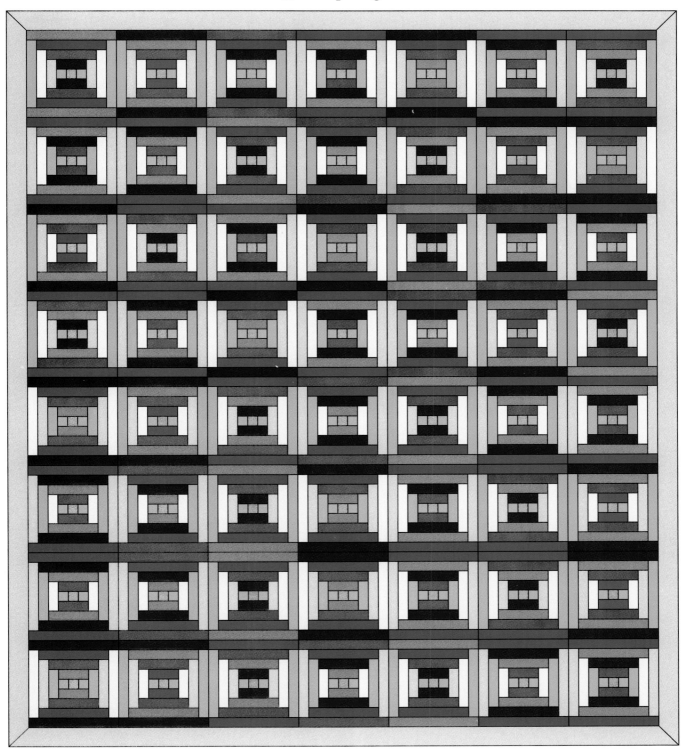

CLAY'S CHOICE COLLECTION

A respected Kentucky statesman of the 1800's, Henry Clay served more than 30 years in the U.S. Congress. His commitment to preserving the Union played a key role in reaching the Missouri Compromise and the Compromise of 1850. But his opposition to slavery ultimately cost him his dream of the presidency. He stood firm in his convictions, stating, "I would rather be right than be president." Quilters of the day were inspired by his bold resolve and honored him with the naming of the Clay's Choice quilt pattern. For our calico version of the traditional design, we used easy grid-pieced triangle-squares to create the simple stars. Plain borders are offset with an inner border of small plain squares set on point.

The old-fashioned look of this pieced star motif inspired a roomful of decorative flair. Elements from the Clay's Choice quilt are assembled on a smaller scale to create a matching wall hanging (opposite). For unusual accents, we used the quilt blocks in a framed accent (left) and a charming bench pad (below).

CLAY'S CHOICE QUILT

SKILL LEVEL: 1 2 3 4 5
BLOCK SIZE: 8" x 8"
QUILT SIZE: 91" x 107"

Because of the quick methods used to duplicate the scrappy look of our quilt, you will have some pieces left over after assembling the blocks.

YARDAGE REQUIREMENTS
Yardage is based on 45"w fabric.

- 6⅞ yds of black print
- 4⅞ yds of cream solid
- 2⅛ yds of yellow print
- ¾ yd *each* of 2 red, 2 blue, and 2 green prints
  8¼ yds for backing
  1 yd for binding
  120" x 120" batting

CUTTING OUT THE PIECES
All measurements include a ¼" seam allowance. Follow **Rotary Cutting**, *page 146, to cut fabric.*

1. **From black print:**
   - Cut 6 strips 22"w. From these strips, cut 12 **rectangles** 16" x 22" for triangle-squares.
   - Cut 2 lengthwise **side outer borders** 3½" x 104".
   - Cut 2 lengthwise **top/bottom outer borders** 3½" x 94".
   - Cut 2 lengthwise **side inner borders** 3½" x 92".
   - Cut 2 lengthwise **top/bottom inner borders** 3½" x 82".

2. **From cream solid:**
   - Cut 25 strips 2½"w. From these strips, cut 396 **small squares** 2½" x 2½".
   - Cut 3 strips 22"w. From these strips, cut 6 **rectangles** 16" x 22" for triangle-square A's.
   - Cut 7 strips 4¼"w. From these strips, cut 59 squares 4¼" x 4¼". Cut squares twice diagonally to make 236 **border triangles**.

3. **From yellow print:**
   - Cut 25 strips 2½"w. From these strips, cut 396 **small squares** 2½" x 2½".

4. **From red, blue, and green prints:**
   - Cut 2 strips 2⅝"w from *each* fabric. From these strips, cut a total of 118 **border squares** 2⅝" x 2⅝".
   - Cut 1 **rectangle** 16" x 22" from *each* fabric for triangle-square B's.

ASSEMBLING THE QUILT TOP
Follow **Piecing and Pressing**, *page 148, to make quilt top.*

1. To make triangle-square A's, place 1 black and 1 cream **rectangle** right sides together. Referring to **Fig. 1**, follow **Making Triangle-Squares**, page 148, to make 70 **triangle-square A's**. Repeat with remaining black and cream **rectangles** to make a total of 420 **triangle-square A's**. (You will need a total of 396 **triangle-square A's**.)

Fig. 1

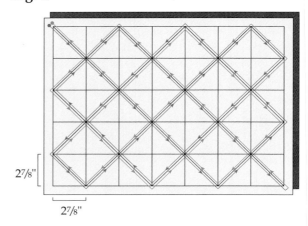

triangle-square A (make 420)

2. To make triangle-square B's, place 1 red and 1 black **rectangle** right sides together. Referring to **Fig. 1**, this page, follow **Making Triangle-Squares**, page 148, to make 70 **triangle-square B's**. Repeat with remaining **rectangles** to make a total of 420 **triangle-square B's**, 70 from each color combination. (You will need 1 set of 4 matching **triangle-square B's** for *each* of the 99 blocks needed for the quilt.)

triangle-square B (make 70 of each)

3. Sew 1 **small square** and 1 **triangle-square A** together to make **Unit 1**. Make 4 **Unit 1's**.

Unit 1 (make 4)

4. Sew 4 matching **triangle-square B's** together to make 1 **Unit 2**.

Unit 2 (make 1)

5. Sew 2 **Unit 1's** and **Unit 2** together to make 1 **Unit 3**.

Unit 3 (make 1)

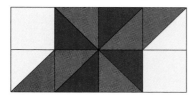

6. Sew 2 **small squares** and 1 **Unit 1** together to make **Unit 4**. Make 2 **Unit 4's**.

Unit 4 (make 2)

7. Sew 2 **Unit 4's** and **Unit 3** together to make 1 **Block**.

Block

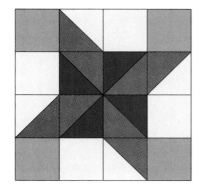

8. Repeat Steps 3 - 7 to make a total of 99 **Blocks**.
9. Referring to **Quilt Top Diagram**, page 100, sew **Blocks** together into rows. Sew rows together to make center section of quilt top.
10. Follow **Adding Squared Borders**, page 151, to sew **side**, then **top** and **bottom inner borders** to center section.
11. Sew 1 **border square** and 2 **border triangles** together to make **Border Unit**. Make 114 **Border Units**.

Border Unit (make 114)

12. Sew 1 **border square** and 2 **border triangles** together to make **Corner Border Unit**. Make 4 **Corner Border Units**.

Corner Border Unit (make 4)

13. In random color order, sew 26 **Border Units** and 1 **Corner Border Unit** together to make **Top/Bottom Pieced Border**. Make 2 **Top/Bottom Pieced Borders**.

Top/Bottom Pieced Border (make 2)

14. Sew 31 **Border Units** and 1 **Corner Border Unit** together to make **Side Pieced Border**. Make 2 **Side Pieced Borders**.

Side Pieced Border (make 2)

15. Follow Steps 1 - 3 of **Adding Mitered Borders**, page 151, to sew **Pieced Borders** to top, bottom, and sides of center section of quilt top.
16. To complete stitching at corners, fold 1 corner of quilt top diagonally with right sides together, matching outer edges of **Pieced Borders** as shown in **Fig. 2**. Beginning at point where previous seams end, sew borders together, backstitching at beginning and end of seam.

Fig. 2

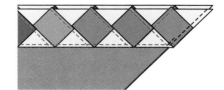

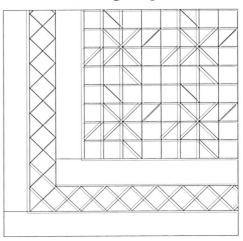

17. Repeat Step 16 to sew remaining **Pieced Border** corners together.
18. Follow **Adding Squared Borders**, page 151, to sew **side**, then **top** and **bottom outer borders** to center section to complete **Quilt Top**.

COMPLETING THE QUILT

1. Follow **Quilting**, page 152, to mark, layer, and quilt using **Quilting Diagram** as a suggestion. Our quilt is hand quilted.
2. Cut a 33" square of binding fabric. Follow **Binding**, page 154, to bind quilt using 2¹⁄₂"w bias binding with mitered corners.

Quilt Top Diagram

CLAY'S CHOICE WALL HANGING

SKILL LEVEL: 1 2 3 4 5
BLOCK SIZE: 8" x 8"
WALL HANGING SIZE: 49" x 49"

YARDAGE REQUIREMENTS

Yardage is based on 45"w fabric.

- ■ 1⁷/₈ yds black print
- ☐ 1³/₈ yds of cream solid
- ▨ ³/₈ yd of yellow print
- ◣ 1 fat quarter (18" x 22" piece) *each* of 2 red, 2 blue, and 2 green prints
- 3 yds for backing and hanging sleeve
- ³/₄ yd for binding
- 52" x 52" batting

CUTTING OUT THE PIECES

All measurements include a ¹/₄" seam allowance. Follow Rotary Cutting, page 146, to cut fabric.

1. **From black print:** ■
   - Cut 1 strip 10"w. From this strip, cut 6 **rectangles** 7" x 10" for triangle-square B's.
   - Cut 2 lengthwise **side outer borders** 3¹/₂" x 48¹/₂".
   - Cut 2 lengthwise **top/bottom outer borders** 3¹/₂" x 42¹/₂".
   - Cut 2 lengthwise **side inner borders** 2¹/₂" x 36¹/₂".
   - Cut 2 lengthwise **top/bottom inner borders** 2¹/₂" x 32¹/₂".
   - Cut 1 **large rectangle** 16" x 22" for triangle-square A's.

2. **From cream solid:** ☐
   - Cut 4 strips 2¹/₂"w. From these strips, cut 64 **small squares** 2¹/₂" x 2¹/₂".
   - Cut 3 strips 4¹/₂"w. From these strips, cut 26 squares 4¹/₂" x 4¹/₂". Cut squares twice diagonally to make 104 **border triangles**.
   - Cut 1 **large rectangle** 16" x 22" for triangle-square A's.

3. **From yellow print:** ▨
   - Cut 4 strips 2¹/₂"w. From these strips, cut 64 **small squares** 2¹/₂" x 2¹/₂".

4. **From red, blue, and green prints:** ◣
   - Cut 1 **rectangle** 7" x 10" from *each* fabric for triangle-square B's.
   - Cut 2 strips 2⁵/₈" x 18" from *each* fabric. From these strips, cut a total of 52 **border squares** 2⁵/₈" x 2⁵/₈".

ASSEMBLING THE WALL HANGING TOP

Follow Piecing and Pressing, page 148, to make wall hanging top.

1. Using **large rectangles**, follow Step 1 of **Assembling the Quilt Top**, page 98, to make 70 **triangle-square A's**. (You will need 64 and have 6 left over.)

triangle-square A (make 70)

2. To make triangle-square B's, place 1 red and 1 black **rectangle** right sides together. Referring to **Fig. 1**, follow **Making Triangle-Squares**, page 148, to make 12 **triangle-square B's**. Repeat with remaining **rectangles** to make a total of 72 **triangle-square B's**, 12 from each color combination. (You will need 1 set of 4 matching **triangle-square B's** for *each* of the 16 blocks needed for the wall hanging.)

Fig. 1

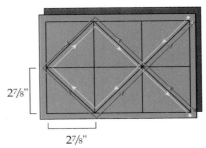

2⁷/₈"

2⁷/₈"

triangle-square B (make 12 of each)

3. Follow Steps 3 - 7 of **Assembling the Quilt Top**, page 98, to make a total of 16 **Blocks**.
4. Referring to **Wall Hanging Top Diagram**, page 102, sew **Blocks** together into rows. Sew rows together to make center section of wall hanging top.
5. Sew **top**, **bottom**, then **side inner borders** to center section.
6. Follow Step 11 of **Assembling the Quilt Top**, page 99, to make 48 **Border Units**.
7. Follow Step 12 of **Assembling the Quilt Top**, page 99, to make 4 **Corner Border Units**.

8. In random color order, sew 12 **Border Units** and 1 **Corner Border Unit** together to make **Pieced Border**. Make 4 **Pieced Borders**.

Pieced Border (make 4)

9. Follow Steps 15 - 17 of **Assembling the Quilt Top**, page 99, to sew **Pieced Borders** to center section.
10. Sew **top**, **bottom**, then **side outer borders** to center section to complete **Wall Hanging Top**.

COMPLETING THE WALL HANGING

1. Follow **Quilting**, page 152, to mark, layer, and quilt wall hanging using **Quilting Diagram**, page 100, as a suggestion. Our wall hanging is hand quilted.
2. Follow **Making a Hanging Sleeve**, page 156, to attach hanging sleeve to wall hanging.
3. Cut a 24" square of binding fabric. Follow **Binding**, page 154, to bind wall hanging using 2¹/₂"w bias binding with mitered corners.

Wall Hanging Top Diagram

BENCH PAD

BENCH PAD SIZE: 16" x 32"

YARDAGE REQUIREMENTS
Yardage is based on 45"w fabric.

1 yd of black print
³/₈ yd of cream solid
¹/₈ yd of yellow print
scraps of red, blue, and green prints
3 yds of 3"w bias strip for welting
3 yds of ¹/₄" cord for welting

You will also need:
14" x 30" piece of 1" foam rubber

CUTTING OUT THE PIECES
*All measurements include a ¹/₄" seam allowance unless otherwise indicated. Follow **Rotary Cutting**, page 146, to cut fabric.*

1. **From black print fabric:**
   • Cut 2 **top/bottom borders** 4¹/₈" x 31³/₄".
   • Cut 2 **side borders** 4¹/₈" x 8¹/₂".
   • Cut 1 **backing** 15¹/₄" x 31³/₄".
   • Cut 1 **rectangle** 7" x 10" for triangle-square A's.
   • Cut 3 **small rectangles** 4" x 7" for triangle-square B's.

2. **From cream solid fabric:**
   • Cut 1 strip 2¹/₂"w. From this strip cut 12 **small squares** 2¹/₂" x 2¹/₂".
   • Cut 1 **rectangle** 7" x 10" for triangle-square A's.

3. **From yellow print fabric:**
   • Cut 1 strip 2¹/₂"w. From this strip, cut 12 **small squares** 2¹/₂" x 2¹/₂".

4. **From red, blue, and green print fabrics:**
   • Cut 1 **small rectangle** 4" x 7" from *each* fabric for triangle-square B's.

MAKING THE BENCH PAD
*Follow **Piecing and Pressing**, page 148, to make bench pad.*

1. To make triangle-square A's, place black and cream **rectangles** right sides together. Referring to **Fig. 1** of **Assembling the Wall Hanging Top**, page 101, follow **Making Triangle-Squares**, page 148, to make 12 **triangle-square A's**.

triangle-square A (make 12)

2. To make triangle-square B's, place red and 1 black **small rectangle** right sides together. Referring to **Fig. 1**, follow **Making Triangle-Squares**, page 148, to make 4 **triangle-square B's**. Repeat with remaining **small rectangles** to make a total of 12 **triangle-square B's**, 4 from each color combination.

Fig. 1

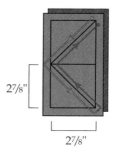

2⁷/₈"

2⁷/₈"

triangle-square B (make 4 of each)

3. Follow Steps 3 - 7 of **Assembling the Quilt Top**, page 98, to make 1 **Block** from each color combination.

Blocks (make 1 of each)

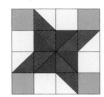

4. Referring to **Bench Pad Top Diagram**, sew **Blocks** together to make center section of bench pad.
5. Sew **side**, then **top** and **bottom borders** to center section to make **Bench Pad Top**.
6. Using a 1/2" seam allowance, follow **Pillow Finishing**, page 157, to complete **Bench Pad** with welting.

Bench Pad Top Diagram

FRAMED BLOCK

SUPPLIES

scraps of black print, red print, yellow print, and cream solid fabrics
picture frame and acid-free mat large enough to accommodate an 8 1/2" block
12" x 12" fabric square for backing
12" x 12" batting
1 1/8 yds of 1 3/4"w bias fabric strip for binding

MAKING THE FRAMED BLOCK

All measurements include a 1/4" seam allowance. Follow ***Rotary Cutting***, *page 146, and* ***Piecing and Pressing***, *page 148, to make block.*

1. Cut 2 **rectangles** 4" x 7" from black print fabric. Cut 1 **rectangle** 4" x 7" *each* from cream solid fabric and red print fabric.
2. To make triangle-square A's, place cream and 1 black **rectangle** right sides together. Referring to **Fig. 1** of **Making the Bench Pad**, follow **Making Triangle-Squares**, page 148, to make 4 **triangle-square A's**. Repeat using remaining **rectangles** to make 4 **triangle-square B's**.

triangle-square A (make 4)

triangle-square B (make 4)

3. Cut 4 **small squares** 2 1/2" x 2 1/2" *each* from yellow print fabric and cream solid fabric.
4. Follow Steps 3 - 7 of **Assembling the Quilt Top**, page 98, to make **Block**.
5. Follow **Quilting**, page 152, to mark, layer, and quilt block using **Quilting Diagram**, page 100, as a suggestion. Our block is hand quilted.
6. Using bias fabric strip, follow **Binding**, page 154, to bind block with mitered corners.
7. Frame block as desired.

HOME SWEET FOLK ART

An early American folk art, the
penny rug was a favorite accent during
a time when rugs were used to cover
tables and beds — not floors, as we
would expect today. The picturesque
designs were pieced with wool felt and
often echoed the quilt appliqués of the
day, such as leaves, flowers, animals,
stars, and other scenes from nature.
We revived this bit of creative history
for our homespun sampler, which
features folksy appliqués surrounding
a lone cottage motif. Embellished
with basic embroidery stitches and
contrasting buttons, this accent
will lend the charm of simplicity
to your "Home Sweet Home."

The woodsy motifs from our wall hanging can also lend a home-style touch to purchased clothing. Add a hint of old-fashioned romance to a felt vest (opposite) with sweet heart and posy accents. For added appeal, complete the vest with the look of prairie point edgings. A special "some-bunny" will hop for this cozy sweatshirt! The bunny appliqué is embellished with button flowers and ribbon. Dress up a plain wool jacket (below) with a field of penny rug flowers. A scalloped border accentuates the collar and cuffs.

"HOME SWEET HOME" WALL HANGING

WALL HANGING SIZE: 23½" x 24"

YARDAGE REQUIREMENTS

Wool felt is available in 60"w or 72"w yardage and in 9" x 12" precut pieces.

- ¾ yd of tan felt
- ¼ yd of dark red felt
- 9" x 12" pieces of felt in assorted colors for appliqués scrap of wool plaid for house appliqué

You will also need:
assorted buttons
embroidery floss to coordinate with felt colors
water-soluble marker
paper-backed fusible web
tracing paper

CUTTING OUT THE PIECES

1. **From tan:**
   - Cut 2 pieces 23½" x 24" for **top** and **back**.
   - Cut 1 **hanging sleeve** 3" x 24".

2. **From dark red:**
   - Cut 4 **borders** 1" x 24½".

3. **From assorted colors:**
   - Referring to **Wall Hanging Top Diagram** use patterns, pages 109 - 111, and follow **Preparing Fusible Appliqués**, page 150, to make the following **appliqués**:

2 **large flowers**	2 **large centers**
8 **medium flowers**	8 **medium centers**
1 **small flower**	1 **small center**
1 **small center circle**	11 **large leaves**
5 **medium leaves**	2 **small leaves**
1 **tree**	1 **rabbit**
1 **large star**	1 **small star**
1 **vase**	1 **vase trim**
1 **large triangle**	4 **small triangles**
1 **heart**	1 **zigzag heart**
2 **birds**	2 **wings**
1 **gable**	2 **windows** ¾" x 1"
1 **roof**	1 **background** 6" x 7¾"
1 **house end** 1¼" x 2½"	
1 **house front** 2½" x 3¼"	

MAKING THE WALL HANGING

*Refer to photo and **Wall Hanging Top Diagram** to make Wall Hanging. Use 3 strands of floss for embroidery unless otherwise indicated.*

1. Cut 4 strips of fusible web 1" x 24½". Trace **scallop** pattern, page 110, onto paper side of each strip, repeating along length of strip. Follow manufacturer's instructions to fuse 1 web strip to one side of each **border**. Cut along scalloped line. Remove paper backing.

2. Fuse side, then top and bottom **borders** on wall hanging **top** 2" from outer edges. Trim ends of borders as needed.

3. Use water-soluble marker to draw a vertical line 5¼" from straight edge of each side **border** and a horizontal line 6¼" from straight edge of top **border** and bottom **border**.

4. Layer and arrange **appliqués** on wall hanging **top**; fuse in place. Trace words, "Home Sweet Home," page 111, onto tracing paper. Pin paper to area above house.

5. Follow **Embroidery Stitches**, page 158, and refer to **Stitch Diagram** to add embroidery details to appliqués and to work running stitch over marked lines, words, and for flower stems. Work **Straight Stitches**, page 158, for birds' beaks. Do not add cross stitches to **borders** at this time. Carefully tear away paper.

6. Matching wrong sides and raw edges, layer wall hanging **top** and **back**. Work running stitch along side and bottom edges. Pin hanging sleeve to back, matching top and side raw edges. Use a running stitch to sew all three layers together along top edge.

7. Use 6 strands of floss to work a cross stitch in the middle of each scallop on **borders**, catching bottom edge of hanging sleeve on top **border**.

8. Embellish with buttons as desired.

APPLIQUÉD CLOTHING

SUPPLIES

wool blazer, sweatshirt, or felt vest
¼ yd pieces or 9" x 12" pieces of wool felt in assorted colors for appliqués
assorted buttons
embroidery floss to coordinate with felt colors
paper-backed fusible web

TRIMMING A GARMENT

1. Referring to photo for suggestions, use patterns, pages 109 - 111, and follow **Preparing Fusible Appliqués**, page 150, to make desired appliqués from felt.
   - For scalloped trim on blazer lapel and cuffs, measure each edge to be trimmed. Cut a strip of web and felt for each edge 1"w x determined measurement. Follow Step 1 of **Making the Wall Hanging**, this page, to trace, fuse, and cut trim. Fuse trim to lapel and cuffs.
   - For sawtooth lining on vest, pin vest front on felt piece leaving ¾" outside vest front edge. Cut out felt piece ½" outside front, bottom, and armhole edges. Cut piece even with shoulder and side seams. Use 3 strands of floss

and **Running Stitch**, page 158, to sew pieces together along front, bottom, and armhole edges. Use scissors to cut sawtooth edge on lining. Repeat for remaining side.

2. Arrange **appliqués** on garment; fuse in place.
3. Using **Stitch Diagram** as a suggestion, embellish appliqués with **Embroidery Stitches**, page 158, and buttons.

Wall Hanging Top Diagram

Stitch Diagram

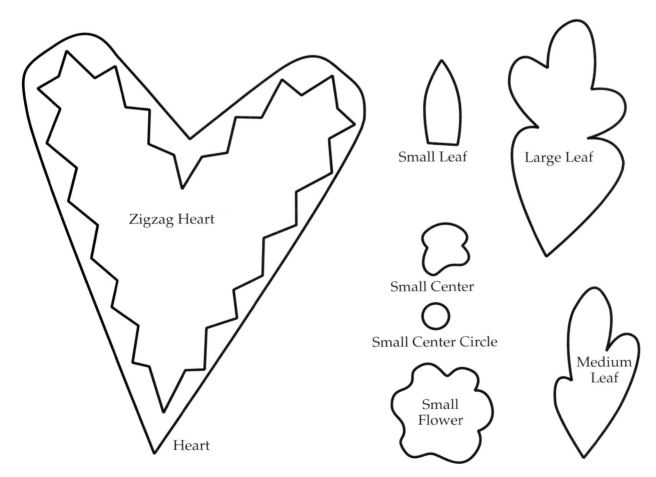

Zigzag Heart

Heart

Small Leaf

Large Leaf

Small Center

Small Center Circle

Small Flower

Medium Leaf

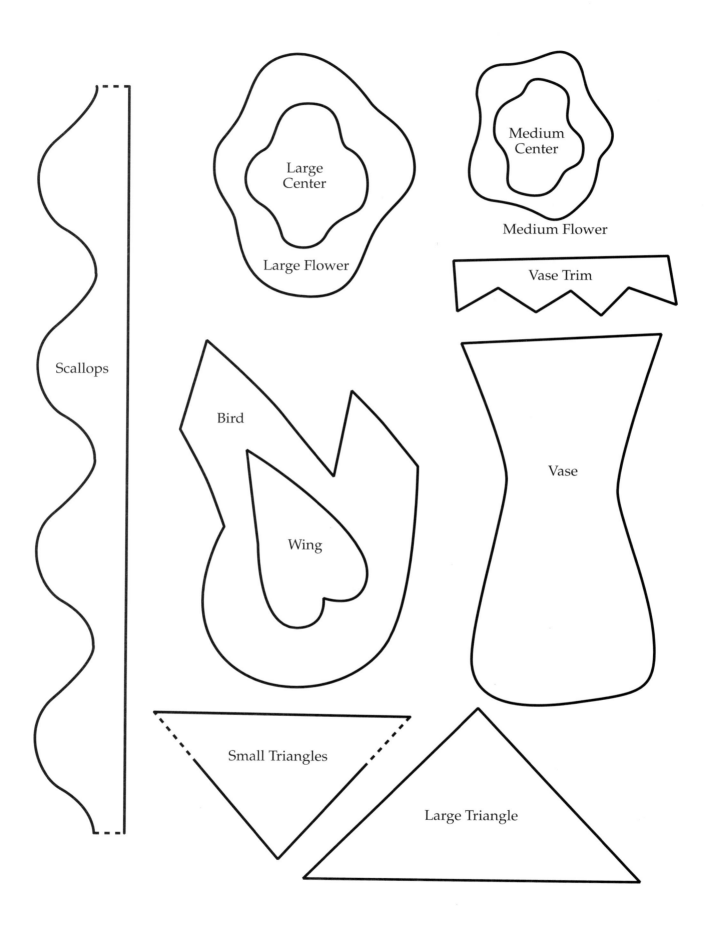

Scallops

Large Center

Large Flower

Medium Center

Medium Flower

Vase Trim

Bird

Wing

Vase

Small Triangles

Large Triangle

110

Home Sweet Home

Gable

Roof

Small Star

Large Star

Tree

Rabbit

LONE STAR LOG CABIN

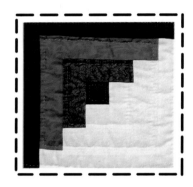

Two time-honored classics of patchwork quilting — the Lone Star and the Log Cabin patterns — join to form a dazzling display of rich color. Featured in the quilt's center medallion, the star motif is made with rows of diamond pieces that are easy to cut from strip-pieced sets. The Log Cabin units are arranged around the medallion in the Barn Raising setting, which radiates rays of light and dark values. Each block is pieced around a center square with the strips cut to size as you go. The rich reds and greens of the quilt are accented by the floral print of the deep outer border.

LONE STAR LOG CABIN QUILT

SKILL LEVEL: 1 2 3 4 5
BLOCK SIZE: 9⅝" x 9⅝"
QUILT SIZE: 99" x 118"

YARDAGE REQUIREMENTS
Yardage is based on 45"w fabric.

☐ 5 yds **total** of assorted cream prints

▨ 4½ yds of black print

■ 3⅛ yds of green solid

▨ 1¼ yds of green print

■ 1 yd of pink print

■ 1 yd of grey print

■ ¾ yd of blue print

■ ⅝ yd of teal print
8¾ yds for backing
1 yd for binding
120" x 120" batting

CUTTING OUT THE PIECES
All measurements include a ¼" seam allowance. Follow Rotary Cutting, page 146, to cut fabric.

1. **From assorted cream prints:** ☐
    * Cut 58 **narrow strips** 1⅞"w.
    * Cut 2 strips 11"w. From these strips, cut 4 **squares** 11" x 11".
    * Cut 1 square 16" x 16". Cut square twice diagonally to make 4 **triangles**.

2. **From black print :** ▨
    * Cut 17 **narrow strips** 1⅞"w.
    * Cut 3 **wide strips** 2⅜"w.
    * Cut 2 lengthwise **side outer borders** 8¼" x 106".
    * Cut 2 lengthwise **top/bottom outer borders** 8¼" x 102.

3. **From green solid:** ■
    * Cut 4 lengthwise **medallion borders** 2¼" x 47½".
    * Cut 2 lengthwise **side inner borders** 3" x 101".
    * Cut 2 lengthwise **top/bottom inner borders** 3" x 87".
    * From remaining fabric width, cut 4 strips 1⅞"w. From these strips, cut 68 **center squares** 1⅞" x 1⅞".

4. **From green print:** ▨
    * Cut 17 **narrow strips** 1⅞"w.
    * Cut 2 **wide strips** 2⅜"w.

5. **From pink print:** ■
    * Cut 12 **narrow strips** 1⅞"w.
    * Cut 3 **wide strips** 2⅜"w.

6. **From grey print:** ■
    * Cut 12 **narrow strips** 1⅞"w.
    * Cut 4 **wide strips** 2⅜"w.

7. **From blue print:** ■
    * Cut 8 **narrow strips** 1⅞"w.
    * Cut 3 **wide strips** 2⅜"w.

8. **From teal print:** ■
    * Cut 8 **narrow strips** 1⅞"w.
    * Cut 1 **wide strip** 2⅜"w.

ASSEMBLING THE QUILT TOP
Follow Piecing and Pressing, page 148, to make quilt top.

1. Sew **wide strips** together in color order shown, adding each new strip 1⅞" from end of previous strip, to make 1 *each* of **Strip Sets A, B, C,** and **D**.

Strip Set A
(make 1)

Strip Set B
(make 1)

Strip Set C
(make 1)

Strip Set D
(make 1)

2. Referring to **Fig. 1**, use a large right-angle triangle aligned with a seam to determine an accurate 45° cutting line. Use rotary cutting equipment to trim the uneven ends from 1 end of each **Strip Set**.

Fig. 1

3. Aligning 45° mark (shown in pink) on rotary cutting ruler with a seam and aligning 2⅜" mark with cut edge made in Step 2, cut across **Strip Sets** at 2⅜" intervals as shown in **Fig. 2**.

Fig. 2

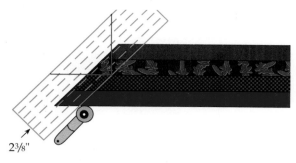

2³⁄₈"

From **Strip Set A**, cut 8 **Unit 1's**. From **Strip Set B**, cut 8 **Unit 2's**. From **Strip Set C**, cut 8 **Unit 3's**. From **Strip Set D**, cut 8 **Unit 4's**.

Unit 1 (cut 8)	Unit 2 (cut 8)	Unit 3 (cut 8)	Unit 4 (cut 8)

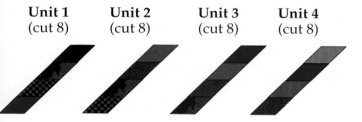

4. To make **Unit 5's**, refer to **Fig. 3** to match long edges of units. Seams will cross ¹⁄₄" from cut edges of fabric. Pin and stitch as shown in **Fig. 3**. Sew 1 **Unit 1**, 1 **Unit 2**, 1 **Unit 3**, and 1 **Unit 4** together in order shown to make **Unit 5**. Make 8 **Unit 5's**.

Fig. 3

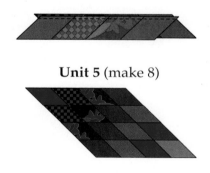

Unit 5 (make 8)

5. To make **Unit 6**, place 2 **Unit 5's** right sides together, carefully matching edges and seams; pin. Stitch in direction shown in **Fig. 4**, ending stitching ¹⁄₄" from edge of fabric (it may be helpful to mark a small dot at this point before sewing) and backstitching at end of seam. Make 4 **Unit 6's**.

Fig. 4

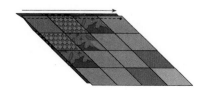

Unit 6 (make 4)

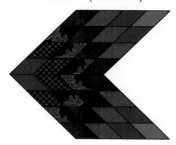

6. Referring to **Star Medallion** diagram, sew **Unit 6's** together to make **Star**, ending stitching ¹⁄₄" from edges and backstitching at end of each seam.
7. Follow Steps 2 - 4 of **Working with Diamonds and Set-in Seams**, page 149, to sew **triangles**, then **squares** to **Star** to make **Star Medallion**.

Star Medallion

8. Place 1 cream **narrow strip** on 1 **center square** with right sides together and matching raw edges. Stitch as shown in **Fig. 5a**. Trim **strip** even with **center square** (**Fig. 5b**); press open (**Fig. 5c**).

Fig. 5a   **Fig. 5b**   **Fig. 5c**

115

9. Turn **square** ¼ turn to the right. Using same cream **narrow strip**, repeat Step 8 to add next "log" as shown in **Figs. 6a - 6c**.

Fig. 6a   **Fig. 6b**   **Fig. 6c**

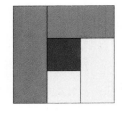

10. Repeat Step 9, adding teal print logs to remaining 2 sides of **square** (**Fig. 7**).

Fig. 7

11. Referring to **Block A** diagram, continue adding logs, alternating 2 matching cream **narrow strips** and 2 grey print **narrow strips**, then 2 matching cream **narrow strips** and 2 black print **narrow strips** to make **Block A**. (There will be 3 logs on each side of **center square**). Make 34 **Block A's**.

Block A (make 34)

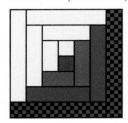

12. Using assorted cream print, blue print, pink print, and green print **narrow strips**, refer to **Block B** diagram for color placement and repeat Steps 8 - 11 to make 34 **Block B's**.

Block B (make 34)

13. Sew 8 **Block A's** and 9 **Block B's** together to make **Quarter Section A**. Make 2 **Quarter Section A's**.

Quarter Section A (make 2)

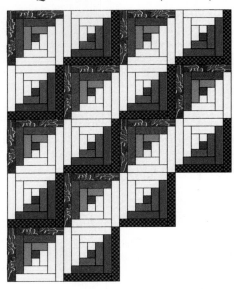

14. Sew 9 **Block A's** and 8 **Block B's** together to make **Quarter Section B**. Make 2 **Quarter Section B's**.

Quarter Section B (make 2)

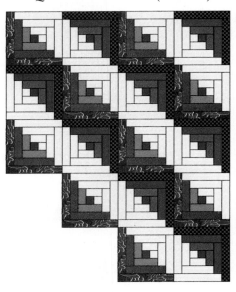

15. To trim diagonal edge of 1 **Quarter Section A**, refer to **Fig. 8** to align ¼" marking on ruler (shown in pink) with diagonal of each center square along uneven edge of **Quarter Section**. Trim off excess. (*Note:* Handle bias edge with care to avoid stretching.) Repeat for remaining **Quarter Sections**.

Fig. 8

Fig. 10

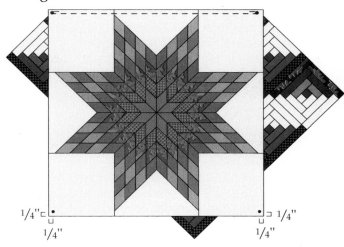

16. Mark center of 1 long edge of 1 **star border**. Mark center of diagonal edge of 1 **Quarter Section**. Matching right sides, center marks, and long raw edges, pin **medallion border** to **Quarter Section**. Sew **medallion border** to **Quarter Section**. Use ruler to trim ends of border even with **Quarter Section** edges (**Fig. 9**). Repeat for remaining **Quarter Sections**.

18. To complete stitching on side, fold quilt top with right sides together, matching outer edges of 2 **Quarter Sections** as shown in **Fig. 11**. Stitch from end of previous stitching to outside edge, backstitching at beginning of seam (**Fig. 11**).

Fig. 9

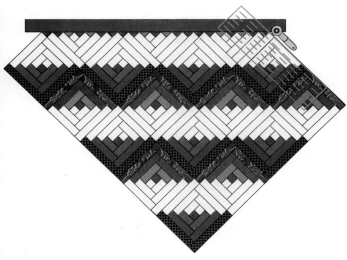

Fig. 11

17. Mark a small dot ¹/₄" from each corner on wrong side of **Star Medallion**. (*Note*: For Steps 17 - 19, refer to Assembly Diagram, page 118.) Sew 1 **Quarter Section** and **Star Medallion** together between dots (**Fig. 10**), backstitching at beginning and end of seam. Repeat to add remaining **Quarter Sections** to **Star Medallion**.

19. Repeat Step 18 for each remaining side to make center section of quilt top.
20. Referring to **Quilt Top Diagram**, page 119, follow **Adding Squared Borders**, page 151, to sew **side**, then **top** and **bottom inner borders** to center section. Repeat to add **outer borders** to complete **Quilt Top**.

COMPLETING THE QUILT

1. Follow **Quilting**, page 152, to mark, layer, and quilt using **Quilting Diagram** as a suggestion. Our quilt is hand quilted.
2. Cut a 34" square of binding fabric. Follow **Binding**, page 154, to bind quilt using 2½"w bias binding with mitered corners.

Quilting Diagram

Assembly Diagram

FRIENDSHIP COLLECTION

Amid the sentimentality of the mid-1800's, the Album quilt emerged as a fashionable way to mark family milestones or honor cherished friendships. Such quilts ranged in style from elaborately appliquéd florals to simple signed patchwork motifs. These priceless quilts were sometimes even pieced with fabrics from the stitchers' own wardrobes, as might have been the case with the antique quilt shown here. For our version of the design, we used easy grid piecing and "sew and flip" methods to create the blocks. The eclectic fabrics are united by the sashing and borders, which are accented with contrasting sashing squares.

Created using a simple papercutting technique, the intertwining hearts of our wall hanging (below) symbolize the special bond between friends who share a love for quilting. The nostalgic Album blocks were pieced with reproduction fabrics, modern prints that re-create patterns from long ago. Signed by the stitchers who made it, the wall hanging will be an endearing wedding present or going-away gift. We added an extra dimension to our papercut appliqué pillows (opposite) with richly textured stipple quilting. Accented with lace, the ruffled pillow offers an inspirational design that's traced onto the fabric using a permanent marker.

Whatsoever thy hand findeth to do, Do it with thy might.
Ecclesiastes 9:10

FRIENDSHIP ALBUM QUILT

SKILL LEVEL: 1 2 3 4 5
BLOCK SIZE: 10½" x 10½"
QUILT SIZE: 82" x 100"

*We simplified the piecing of this quilt by substituting solid setting triangles for the partial blocks used on the edges of our antique quilt (see **Assembly Diagram**, page 126). We also resized the quilt to fit a double or queen bed.*

YARDAGE REQUIREMENTS

Yardage is based on 45"w fabric.

 1 fat quarter (18" x 22" piece) *each* of 16 assorted light prints

1 fat quarter *each* of 16 assorted dark prints

3⅜ yds of green print

1½ yds *total* of assorted light prints for setting pieces

½ yd of yellow print
7½ yds for backing
1 yd for binding
90" x 108" batting

CUTTING OUT THE PIECES

*All measurements include a ¼" seam allowance. Follow **Rotary Cutting**, page 146, to cut fabric.*

Note: Before cutting pieces for blocks, cut *each* light print and *each* dark print fat quarter in half to make 2 **pieces** 11" x 18". Select 1 light print **piece** and 1 dark print **piece** for each block.

1. **From *each* light print piece:**
   - Cut 1 **rectangle** 7" x 9" for triangle-squares.
   - Cut 1 **square** 5½" x 5½".
   - Cut 8 **small squares** 2¼" x 2¼".

2. **From *each* dark print piece:**
   - Cut 1 **rectangle** 7" x 9" for triangle-squares.
   - Cut 2 squares 4½" x 4½". Cut squares once diagonally to make 4 **triangles**.
   - Cut 4 **small rectangles** 2¼" x 4".

3. **From green print:**
   - Cut 2 lengthwise **side borders** 3¼" x 103".
   - Cut 2 lengthwise **top/bottom borders** 3¼" x 85".
   - From remaining fabric width, cut 10 strips 11"w. From these strips, cut 80 **sashing strips** 3¼" x 11".

4. **From assorted light prints:**
   - Cut 4 squares 16⅛" x 16⅛". Cut squares twice diagonally to make 16 **side triangles**. (You will need 14 and have 2 left over.)
   - Cut 2 squares 8⅜" x 8⅜". Cut squares once diagonally to make 4 **corner triangles**.

5. **From yellow print:**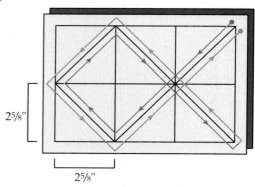
   - Cut 3 strips 3¼"w. From these strips, cut 31 **sashing squares** 3¼" x 3¼".
   - Cut 1 strip 5⅛"w. From this strip, cut 5 squares 5⅛" x 5⅛". Cut squares twice diagonally to make 20 **sashing triangles**. (You will need 18 and have 2 left over.)

ASSEMBLING THE QUILT TOP

*Follow **Piecing and Pressing**, page 148, to make quilt top.*

1. To make triangle-squares, place 1 dark print and 1 light print **rectangle** right sides together. Referring to **Fig. 1**, follow **Making Triangle-Squares**, page 148, to make 12 **triangle-squares**.

Fig. 1

2⅝"

2⅝"

triangle-square (make 12)

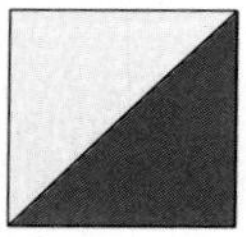

2. Using same color combination as in Step 1, place 1 **small square** on 1 **small rectangle** with right sides together and stitch diagonally as shown in **Fig. 2**. Trim ¼" from stitching line as shown in **Fig. 3**. Press open, pressing seam allowance toward darker fabric.

Fig. 2 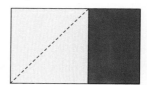 **Fig. 3**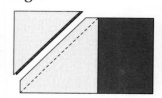

3. Place 1 **small square** on opposite end of **small rectangle**. Stitch diagonally as shown in **Fig. 4**. Trim and press open as in Step 2 to complete **Unit 1**. Make 4 **Unit 1's**.

Fig. 4

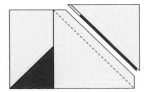

Unit 1 (make 4)

4. Sew 2 **triangle-squares** and 1 **Unit 1** together to make **Unit 2**. Make 4 **Unit 2's**.

Unit 2 (make 4)

5. Sew 2 **triangle-squares** and 1 **Unit 2** together to make **Unit 3**. Make 2 **Unit 3's**.

Unit 3 (make 2)

6. Using same color combination as in Step 1, sew 4 **triangles** and 1 **square** together to make 1 **Unit 4**.

Unit 4 (make 1)

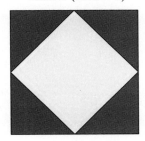

7. Sew 2 **Unit 2's** and **Unit 4** together to make 1 **Unit 5**.

Unit 5 (make 1)

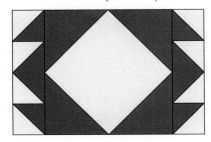

8. Sew 2 **Unit 3's** and **Unit 5** together to make **Block**.

Block

9. Repeat Steps 1 - 8 to make a total of 32 **Blocks**.
10. Referring to **Assembly Diagram**, page 126, sew **corner triangles**, **sashing triangles**, **sashing strips**, **sashing squares**, **side triangles**, and **Blocks** together into diagonal rows. Sew rows together to make center section of quilt top.
11. Follow **Adding Mitered Borders**, page 151, to add **borders** to center section to complete **Quilt Top**.

COMPLETING THE QUILT

1. Follow **Quilting**, page 152, to mark, layer, and quilt using **Quilting Diagram** as a suggestion. Our quilt is hand quilted.
2. Cut a 32" square of binding fabric. Follow **Binding**, page 154, to bind quilt using 2$\frac{1}{2}$"w bias binding with mitered corners.

Quilting Diagram

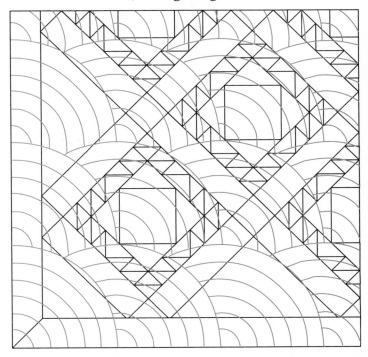

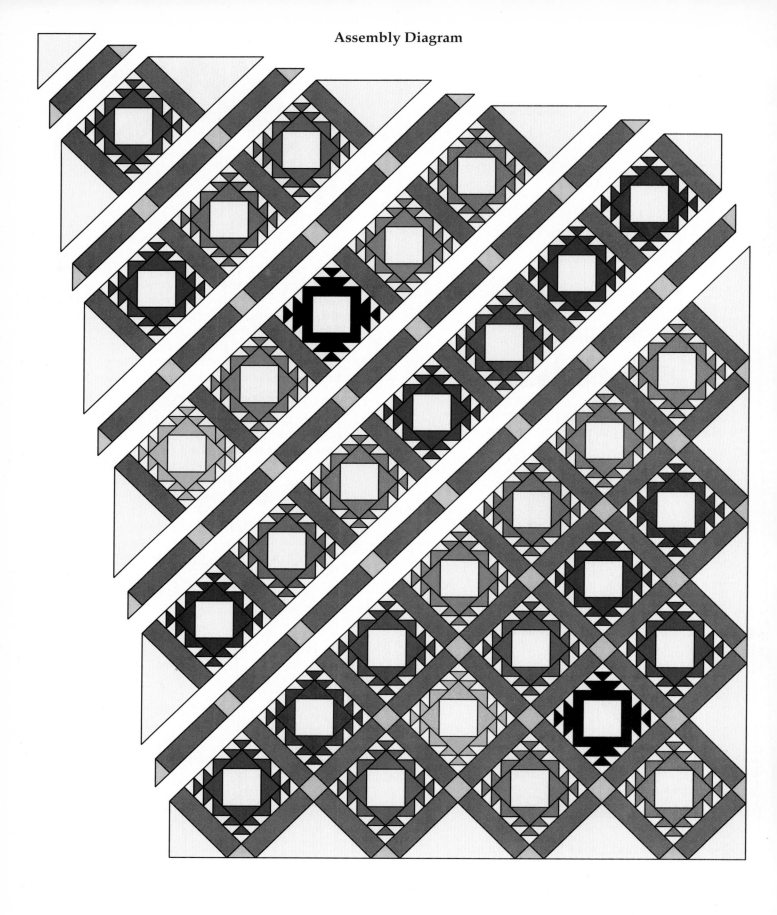

ALBUM WALL HANGING

SKILL LEVEL: 1 2 3 4 5
BLOCK SIZE: 10¹/₂" x 10¹/₂"
WALL HANGING SIZE: 30" x 30"

YARDAGE REQUIREMENTS

Yardage is based on 45"w fabric.

- ⬜ ⁷/₈ yd of light pink print
- ⬛ ⁷/₈ yd of floral print
- ⬛ ³/₈ yd of brown print
- ⬛ ³/₈ yd of dark pink print
- ⬛ ¹/₈ yd of medium pink print
- 1¹/₈ yds for backing and hanging sleeve
- ⁵/₈ yd for binding
- 33" x 33" batting

You will also need:
- 5" x 5" square of freezer paper
- 10" x 10" square of paper-backed fusible web
- transparent monofilament thread for appliqué
- permanent fabric pen

CUTTING OUT THE PIECES

All measurements include a ¹/₄" seam allowance. Follow
Rotary Cutting, page 146, to cut fabric.

1. **From light pink print:** ⬜
    - Cut 1 strip 5¹/₂"w. From this strip, cut 4
      squares 5¹/₂" x 5¹/₂".
    - Cut 2 strips 2¹/₄"w. From these strips, cut 32
      small squares 2¹/₄" x 2¹/₄".
    - Cut 1 **rectangle** 12" x 18" for triangle-squares.

2. **From floral print:** ⬛
    - Cut 1 strip 4¹/₂"w. From this strip, cut 8
      squares 4¹/₂" x 4¹/₂". Cut squares once
      diagonally to make 16 **triangles**.
    - Cut 2 strips 2¹/₄"w. From these strips, cut 16
      small rectangles 2¹/₄" x 4".
    - Cut 1 **rectangle** 12" x 18" for triangle-squares.

3. **From brown print:** ⬛
    - Cut 4 strips 3"w. From these strips, cut 12
      sashing strips 3" x 11".

127

4. From dark pink print:
- Cut 1 **large square** 10" x 10".

5. From medium pink print:
- Cut 1 strip 3"w. From this strip, cut 9 **sashing squares** 3" x 3".

ASSEMBLING THE WALL HANGING TOP

*Follow **Piecing and Pressing**, page 148, to make wall hanging top.*

1. To make triangle-squares, place light pink and floral **rectangles** right sides together. Referring to **Fig. 1**, follow **Making Triangle-Squares**, page 148, to make 48 **triangle-squares**.

Fig. 1

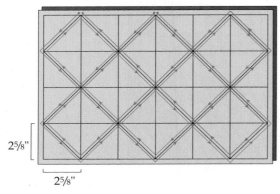

2⅝"
2⅝"

triangle-square (make 48)

2. Using **small squares** and **small rectangles**, follow Steps 2 and 3 of **Assembling the Quilt Top**, page 124, to make 16 **Unit 1's**.

Unit 1 (make 16)

3. Using **triangle-squares**, **Unit 1's**, **squares**, and **triangles**, follow Steps 4 - 8 of **Assembling the Quilt Top**, page 125, to make 4 **Blocks**. (You will need 16 **Unit 2's**, 8 **Unit 3's**, 4 **Unit 4's**, and 4 **Unit 5's**.)

Block (make 4)

4. Follow manufacturer's instructions to fuse web to wrong side of **large square**. Cut large square into 4 **squares** 5" x 5". Do not remove paper backing.

5. To make pattern for appliqué, carefully fold and crease freezer paper, shiny side in, into eighths as shown in **Figs. 2a - 2c** (dots indicate center of paper). Unfold paper and use **Papercut Pattern A**, page 131, to trace pattern onto section shaded in **Fig. 2d**.

Fig. 2a   **Fig. 2b**

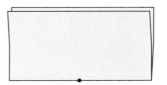

Fig. 2c   **Fig. 2d**

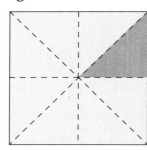

6. Refold paper and use small, sharp scissors to cut out appliqué shape, cutting away shaded sections of pattern. Unfold freezer paper pattern.

7. Center pattern, shiny side down, on wrong side of 1 fused fabric square; use a dry iron to iron pattern in place.

8. Use a sharp pencil to draw around freezer paper pattern; remove pattern. Use small, sharp scissors to carefully cut out **appliqué**. Remove paper backing.

9. Reusing freezer paper pattern each time, repeat Steps 7 and 8 to make 4 **appliqués**.

10. Follow **Invisible Appliqué**, page 150, to fuse and stitch 1 **appliqué** to each **Block**. Use permanent pen to write name on each block in center of appliqué.
11. Sew 3 **sashing squares** and 2 **sashing strips** together to make **Row A**. Make 3 **Row A's**.

Row A (make 3)

12. Sew 3 **sashing strips** and 2 **Blocks** together to make **Row B**. Make 2 **Row B's**.

Row B (make 2)

13. Referring to **Wall Hanging Top Diagram**, sew **Rows** together to complete **Wall Hanging Top**.

COMPLETING THE WALL HANGING
1. Follow **Quilting**, page 152, to mark, layer, and quilt using **Quilting Diagram** as a suggestion. Our wall hanging is hand quilted.
2. Follow **Making a Hanging Sleeve**, page 156, to attach hanging sleeve to wall hanging.
3. Cut a 20" square of binding fabric. Follow **Binding**, page 154, to bind wall hanging using 2¹/₂"w bias binding with mitered corners.

Wall Hanging Top Diagram

Wall Hanging Quilting Diagram

PAPERCUT PILLOW A

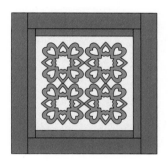

PILLOW SIZE: 17" x 17"

SUPPLIES
10" x 10" **large square** of pink print fabric
10" x 10" square of paper-backed fusible web
5" x 5" square of freezer paper
11¹/₂" x 11¹/₂" **background square** of light pink print fabric
4 **inner borders** 1¹/₄" x 14" of brown print fabric
4 **outer borders** 2¹/₄" x 18" of floral print fabric
19" x 19" square of fabric for pillow top backing
19" x 19" batting
16¹/₂" x 16¹/₂" square of fabric for pillow back
2¹/₂" x 76" bias fabric strip for binding
polyester fiberfill

MAKING THE PILLOW
*Follow **Piecing and Pressing**, page 148, to make pillow.*
1. Follow Steps 4 - 9 of **Assembling the Wall Hanging Top** to make 4 **appliqués** using **Papercut Pattern A**.
2. Arrange appliqués on **background square** and follow manufacturer's instructions to fuse in place.
3. Sew **inner borders** to top, bottom, then side edges of background square, trimming off remainder of each **border** after stitching. Repeat to add **outer borders** to make pillow top.

4. Follow **Quilting**, page 152, to layer and quilt pillow top. The center of our pillow top is machine quilted in a stipple pattern (see **Machine Stipple Quilting**, page 154) with in-the-ditch quilting between the borders.

5. Trim batting and backing even with pillow top. Place pillow top and pillow back wrong sides together; sew pieces together using a 1/4" seam allowance and leaving an opening for stuffing. Stuff pillow with fiberfill and sew opening closed.

6. Fold bias fabric strip in half lengthwise, matching wrong sides and raw edges, and follow **Attaching Binding with Mitered Corners**, page 155, to bind pillow edges.

PAPERCUT PILLOW B

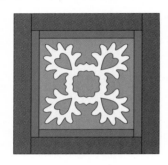

PILLOW SIZE: 16½" x 16½"

SUPPLIES
8½" x 8½" square of light pink print fabric
8½" x 8½" square of paper-backed fusible web
8½" x 8½" square of freezer paper
11" x 11" **background square** of pink print fabric
4 **inner borders** 1¼" x 14" of brown print fabric
4 **outer borders** 2¼" x 18" of floral print fabric
18" x 18" square of fabric for pillow top backing
18" x 18" batting
16" x 16" square of fabric for pillow back
2½" x 72" bias fabric strip for binding
polyester fiberfill

MAKING THE PILLOW
*Follow **Piecing and Pressing**, page 148, to make pillow.*

1. Follow manufacturer's instructions to fuse web to wrong side of light pink fabric. Do not remove paper backing.

2. Use **Papercut Pattern B** and refer to Steps 5 - 8 of **Assembling the Wall Hanging Top**, page 128, to make 1 **appliqué**.

3. Center appliqué on **background square** and follow manufacturer's instructions to fuse in place.

4. Follow Steps 3 - 6 of **Making the Pillow**, page 129, to complete pillow.

HEART PILLOW

PILLOW SIZE: 15½" x 15½" (including ruffle)

SUPPLIES
12" x 12" square of pink print fabric
12" x 12" square of cream print fabric
12" x 12" square of paper-backed fusible web
12" x 12" square of freezer paper
1 yd of ¾"w flat lace
5½" x 80" strip of floral print fabric
    (pieced as necessary) for ruffle
80" of 2"w flat lace
½"w purchased pink ribbon rose
¼ yd of ⅛"w light pink satin ribbon
¼ yd of ¼"w pink satin ribbon
permanent fabric marking pen
polyester fiberfill

MAKING THE PILLOW
1. Place freezer paper, shiny side down, over **Lacy Heart Pattern** and trace.

2. Use a dry iron to iron freezer paper, shiny side down, to wrong side of cream print square. Use fabric marking pen to trace design onto right side of cream print square. Remove freezer paper.

3. Center web square, web side down, over **Lacy Heart Pattern** and trace outer solid outline of heart only. Follow manufacturer's instructions to fuse web to wrong side of pink print square. Carefully cut out heart shape, leaving outer portion of square intact. Remove paper backing.

4. Layer cream print square and pink print square, right sides up, centering heart cutout over heart design. Follow manufacturer's instructions to fuse layers together.

5. Position ¾"w lace around heart, aligning edge of lace with raw edge of heart cutout. Use a narrow zigzag stitch to stitch around heart to secure edges of lace and heart cutout.

6. Trim square to measure 11" x 11" to make **Pillow Top**.

7. Use 5½" x 80" fabric strip and follow Step 2 of **Adding Ruffle to Pillow Top**, page 157, to prepare fabric strip. Repeat using 2"w lace.

8. Aligning raw edges of fabric strip with one edge of 2"w lace, follow Steps 3 and 4 of **Adding Ruffle to Pillow Top** to make ruffle and baste to pillow top.

9. Follow **Pillow Finishing**, page 157, to make pillow.

10. Tie ribbons into a small bow. Tack bow to pillow; tack ribbon rose over bow knot to complete pillow.

Lacy Heart Pattern

Whatever thy hand
findeth to do;
Do it with thy might

Ecclesiastes
9:10

Papercut Pattern B

Papercut Pattern A

COUNTRY CHRISTMAS COLLECTION

Beloved Yuletide images bring festive flair to our winsome holiday wall hanging. Each of the four blocks features a merry motif: a cheery Christmas tree, a heavenly angel, the jolly old gent himself, and a mirthful gingerbread boy. The designs, enhanced by pen-work details, are so easy to appliqué — simply fuse them in place for a no-fuss finish! Surrounding each square is a pieced sawtooth border made using our quick sew-and-flip technique, which gives you perfect points! Complete the scene with a tabletop tree decked with our Christmas cutouts.

Keep your treasured holiday memories safe inside this easy-to-cover album (below) — it's watched over by a blissful fused-on angel appliqué. A sweet embellishment for a purchased long-sleeve T-shirt (opposite), our gingerbread motif is edged by heart cutouts and a checkerboard border.

COUNTRY CHRISTMAS WALL HANGING

SKILL LEVEL: 1 2 3 4 5
BLOCK SIZE: 12" x 12"
WALL HANGING SIZE: 35" x 35"

YARDAGE REQUIREMENTS

Yardage is based on 45"w fabric.

- ■ 1¼ yds of green print
- ◱ ⅞ yd *total* of assorted cream prints
- ◼ ¼ yd *total* of assorted red prints
- ◸ scraps of assorted prints for appliqués
  1¼ yds for backing and hanging sleeve
  ¼ yd for binding
  38" x 38" batting

You will also need:
  paper-backed fusible web
  black permanent fabric pen

CUTTING OUT THE PIECES

All measurements include a ¼" seam allowance. Follow Rotary Cutting, page 146, to cut fabric.

1. **From green print:** ■
   - Cut 2 **side borders** 2½" x 34½".
   - Cut 2 **top/bottom borders** 2½" x 30½".
   - From remaining fabric width, cut 3 strips 4½"w. From these strips, cut 32 **rectangles** 2½" x 4½".

2. **From assorted cream prints:** ◱
   - Cut 4 **background squares** 9" x 9" (1 *each* from 4 different prints).
   - Cut 12 **sashing rectangles** 2½" x 12½" (4 from 1 print, 8 from a different print).
   - Cut 4 strips 2½"w. From these strips, cut 64 matching **squares** 2½" x 2½".

3. **From assorted red prints:** ◼
   - Cut a total of 25 **squares** 2½" x 2½".

PREPARING THE APPLIQUÉS

Referring to Wall Hanging Top Diagram, page 138, and using patterns, pages 141 - 143, and scraps of assorted fabrics, follow Preparing Fusible Appliqués, page 150, to make appliqués.

1. For 1 **Tree Block**, you will need:

1 **tree skirt**	1 **star**
1 **tree bottom**	2 **vines** (1 in reverse)
1 **tree middle**	6 **leaves** (3 in reverse)
1 **treetop**	6 **oval flowers**
5 **tiny trees**	6 **oval flower centers**
3 **small hearts**	8 **dots** (for vine)
2 **tiny gingerbread boys**	

2. For 1 **Angel Block**, you will need:

1 **base**	1 **head**
1 **apron**	1 **hair**
3 **tiny trees**	2 **dots** (for cheeks)
1 **small heart**	1 **swag**
1 **skirt**	4 **leaves** (2 in reverse)
2 **wings** (1 in reverse)	4 **stars**
2 **feet** (1 in reverse)	3 **oval flowers**
2 **hands** (1 in reverse)	3 **oval flower centers**
2 **sleeves** (1 in reverse)	

3. For 1 **Santa Block**, you will need:

1 **Santa coat**	2 **mittens** (1 in reverse)
1 **coat trim**	2 **boots**
2 **cuffs** (1 in reverse)	1 **dot** (for pom-pom)
3 **dots** (for buttons)	1 **ground**
1 **cap**	4 **leaves** (2 in reverse)
1 **cap trim**	1 **small heart**
1 **Santa face**	2 **flowers**
1 **dot** (for nose)	2 **flower centers**
1 **beard**	1 **star**
1 **mustache**	1 **swag**
2 **dots** (for cheeks)	4 **dots** (for berries)
2 **large hearts** (1 in reverse)	

4. For 1 **Gingerbread Boy Block**, you will need:

1 **gingerbread boy**	1 **tree branch**
2 **dots** (for cheeks)	4 **flowers**
1 **jacket** (2 pieces)	4 **flower centers**
1 **cookie base**	1 **small tree**
1 **cookie icing**	5 **leaves** (2 in reverse)
3 **tiny gingerbread boys**	

ASSEMBLING THE WALL HANGING TOP

Follow Piecing and Pressing, page 148, to make wall hanging top.

1. Referring to **Wall Hanging Top Diagram**, page 138, arrange **appliqués** on **background squares**, overlapping as necessary. Follow manufacturer's instructions to fuse in place. Trim **background squares** to 8½" x 8½".

2. Use permanent pen to add eyes and buttons to tiny gingerbread boys, tiny tree trunks, and blanket stitching along edge of tree skirt on **Tree Block**; eyes, mouth, tiny tree trunks, and star ornament hangers on **Angel Block**; arm lines, eyes, mustache details, and berry stems on **Santa Block**; and eyes, mouth, blanket stitching along edges of jacket, and tiny gingerbread boy ornament hangers on **Gingerbread Boy Block**.

3. Place 1 cream print **square** on 1 **rectangle** and stitch diagonally (**Fig. 1**). Trim ¼" from stitching (**Fig. 2**). Press open, pressing seam allowance toward darker fabric.

Fig. 1

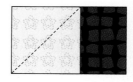

Fig. 2

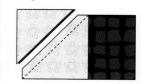

4. Place 1 cream print **square** on opposite end of **rectangle** and stitch diagonally (**Fig. 3**). Trim ¼" from stitching (**Fig. 4**). Press open, pressing seam allowance toward darker fabric, to make **Unit 1**.

Fig. 3   **Fig. 4**

Unit 1

5. Repeat Steps 3 and 4 to make 32 **Unit 1's**.
6. Sew 2 **Unit 1's** together to make **Unit 2**. Make 16 **Unit 2's**.

Unit 2 (make 16)

7. Sew 1 **Unit 2** and 2 red **squares** together to make **Unit 3**. Make 8 **Unit 3's**.

Unit 3 (make 8)

8. Sew 2 **Unit 2's** and 1 appliquéd **background square** together to make **Unit 4**. Repeat with remaining appliquéd **background squares** to make a total of 4 **Unit 4's**.

Unit 4 (make 4)

9. Sew 2 **Unit 3's** and 1 **Unit 4** together to make **Block**. Repeat with remaining **Unit 4's** to make a total of 4 **Blocks**.

Block (make 4)

10. Sew 3 red **squares** and 2 **sashing rectangles** together to make **Sashing Row**. Make 3 **Sashing Rows**.

Sashing Row (make 3)

11. Sew 3 **sashing rectangles** and 2 **Blocks** together to make **Block Row**. Make 2 **Block Rows**.

Block Row (make 2)

12. Referring to **Wall Hanging Top Diagram**, page 138, sew **Sashing Rows** and **Block Rows** together to make center section of wall hanging.
13. Sew **top**, **bottom**, then **side borders** to center section to complete **Wall Hanging Top**.

COMPLETING THE WALL HANGING
1. Follow **Quilting**, page 152, to mark, layer, and quilt using **Quilting Diagram**, page 138, as a suggestion. Our wall hanging is hand quilted.
2. Follow **Making a Hanging Sleeve**, page 156, to attach hanging sleeve to wall hanging.
3. Follow **Binding**, page 154, to bind wall hanging using 2½"w straight-grain binding with overlapped corners.

Wall Hanging Top Diagram

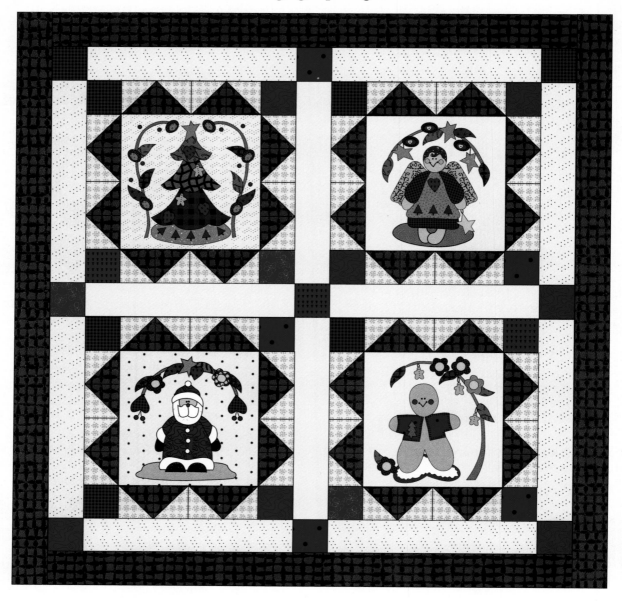

Quilting Diagram

CHRISTMAS ORNAMENTS

SUPPLIES

*For **each** ornament, you will need:*

5¹/₂" x 7" **fabric rectangle** for ornament backing
5¹/₂" x 7" **rectangle** of low-loft cotton batting
scraps of assorted print fabrics for appliqués
paper-backed fusible web
8" length of raffia for hanger
raffia lengths for bow
silk greenery sprig
black permanent fabric pen
hot glue gun and glue sticks

MAKING THE ORNAMENTS

1. Referring to **Ornament Diagrams**, use patterns, pages 141 - 143, and follow **Preparing Fusible Appliqués**, page 150, to make **appliqués** for each ornament.
2. Arrange **appliqués** on batting **rectangle**, overlapping as necessary; fuse in place.
3. Trim batting approximately ¹/₈" outside appliqués.
4. Use permanent pen to add eyes and buttons to tiny gingerbread boys on **Tree**; eyes, mouth, tiny tree trunks, and star hanger to **Angel**; arm lines, eyes, and mustache details to **Santa**; and eyes, mouth, and blanket stitching along edges of jacket to **Gingerbread Boy**.
5. For backing and hanger, trace around ornament, right side up, on paper side of web. Follow manufacturer's instructions to fuse web to wrong side of **fabric rectangle**. Cut out backing along traced line; remove paper backing. Match wrong side of ornament to web side of backing. Place 1" of hanger ends between ornament and backing at top of ornament; fuse layers together.
6. Tie several lengths of raffia into a bow; glue to top of hanger. Glue greenery to knot of bow.

Ornament Diagrams

GINGERBREAD T-SHIRT

SUPPLIES

T-shirt
1 **background square** 7" x 7" of green print fabric
8 **squares** 2¹/₂" x 2¹/₂" of assorted red print fabrics
8 **squares** 2¹/₂" x 2¹/₂" of assorted cream print fabrics
scraps of assorted fabrics for appliqués
paper-backed fusible web
transparent monofilament thread
black permanent fabric pen

TRIMMING THE T-SHIRT

1. Wash, dry, and press T-shirt and fabrics.
2. (*Note:* For Steps 2 - 6, refer to **Block** diagram, page 140). Use patterns, page 142, and follow **Preparing Fusible Appliqués**, page 150, to cut the following appliqués from scrap fabrics:
   - 1 **gingerbread boy**
   - 1 **jacket** (2 pieces)
   - 4 **large hearts**
   - 2 **dots** (for cheeks)
3. Arrange appliqués on **background square**, overlapping as necessary, and follow manufacturer's instructions to fuse in place. Trim background square to 6¹/₂" x 6¹/₂".
4. Sew **squares** together to make 2 **Unit 1's** and 2 **Unit 2's**.

Unit 1

Unit 2

5. Sew **Unit 1's** to top and bottom edges of **background square**. Sew **Unit 2's** to sides of **background square**.
6. Use permanent pen to draw eyes and mouth to complete **Block**.

Block

7. Press raw edges of **Block** 1/4" to wrong side. Cut a 9 3/4" x 9 3/4" square of web. Center and fuse web to wrong side of **Block**; remove paper backing.
8. Position **Block** on front of shirt; fuse in place.
9. Using transparent thread, topstitch along pressed edges of **Block**.

ANGELIC PHOTO ALBUM

YARDAGE REQUIREMENTS
Yardage is based on 45"w fabric.

- 1 yd of red print
- 1/4 yd of cream print
- 1/8 yd of gold print
- scraps of assorted prints for appliqués
  10" x 23" batting

You will also need:
10" x 11 1/2" x 2" photo album
2 pieces 9 1/2"x 10 1/2" of lightweight cardboard
paper-backed fusible web
transparent monofilament thread
black permanent fabric pen
hot glue gun and glue sticks

CUTTING OUT THE PIECES
All measurements include a 1/4" seam allowance. Follow Rotary Cutting, page 146, to cut fabric.

1. **From red print:**
   - Cut 1 **strip** 2"w.
   - Cut 1 **large rectangle** 17 1/2" x 28" for album cover.
   - Cut 2 **small rectangles** 12" x 13 1/2" for inside album covers.

2. **From cream print:**
   - Cut 1 **background square** 7 1/2" x 8 1/2".

3. **From gold print:**
   - Cut 2 **top/bottom borders** 1 1/4" x 7 1/2".
   - Cut 2 **side borders** 1 1/4" x 7 1/2".

MAKING THE ALBUM COVER
Follow Piecing and Pressing, page 148, to make album cover.

1. Follow Step 2 of **Preparing the Appliqués**, page 136, to make angel appliqués. Arrange appliqués on **background square**, overlapping as necessary. Follow manufacturer's instructions to fuse in place. Use permanent pen to add eyes, mouth, and star ornament hanger.
2. Sew **top**, **bottom**, then **side borders** to **background square** to complete **Block**.
3. Press borders 1/4" to wrong side.
4. Matching wrong side of **Block** to right side of **large rectangle**, center **Block** on right-hand side of **large rectangle**; pin in place.
5. Using transparent thread, topstitch along pressed edges of **Block**.

COVERING THE ALBUM
1. With album closed, glue batting to outside of album.
2. Place open album on wrong side of **large rectangle**, centering **Block** on front of album.
3. Fold corners of **large rectangle** diagonally over corners of album; glue in place.
4. Taking care not to distort shape of block on front cover, fold short edges of fabric over side edges of album; glue in place. Fold long edges of fabric over top and bottom edges of album, trimming fabric to fit approximately 1/4" under binding hardware; glue in place.
5. Measure length (top to bottom) of album along hardware. From **strip**, cut 2 **pieces** 1" shorter than determined measurement. Press short ends of each piece 1/4" to wrong side.
6. On inside cover of album, center and glue 1 **piece** along each side of binding hardware with 1 long edge of each **piece** tucked approximately 1/4" under hardware.
7. Center 1 piece of cardboard on wrong side of 1 **small rectangle**. Fold edges of fabric over edges of cardboard; glue in place. Repeat to cover remaining cardboard piece.
8. Center and glue covered cardboard pieces inside front and back covers of album.

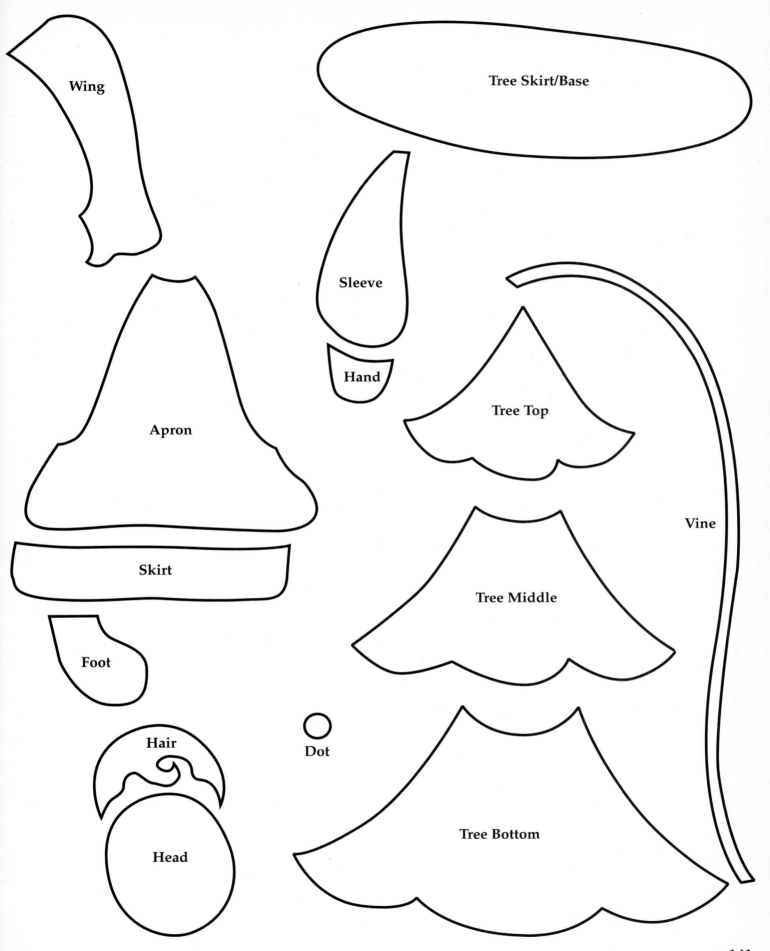

Wing

Tree Skirt/Base

Sleeve

Hand

Apron

Tree Top

Vine

Skirt

Tree Middle

Foot

Dot

Hair

Tree Bottom

Head

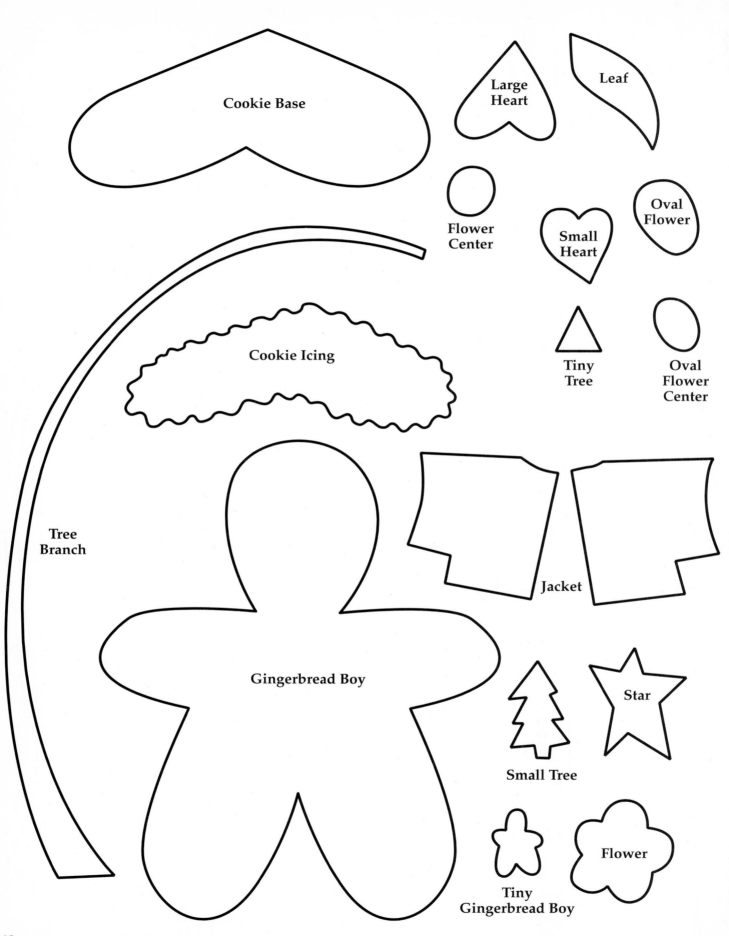

Cookie Base

Large Heart

Leaf

Flower Center

Oval Flower

Small Heart

Cookie Icing

Tiny Tree

Oval Flower Center

Tree Branch

Gingerbread Boy

Jacket

Small Tree

Star

Tiny Gingerbread Boy

Flower

142

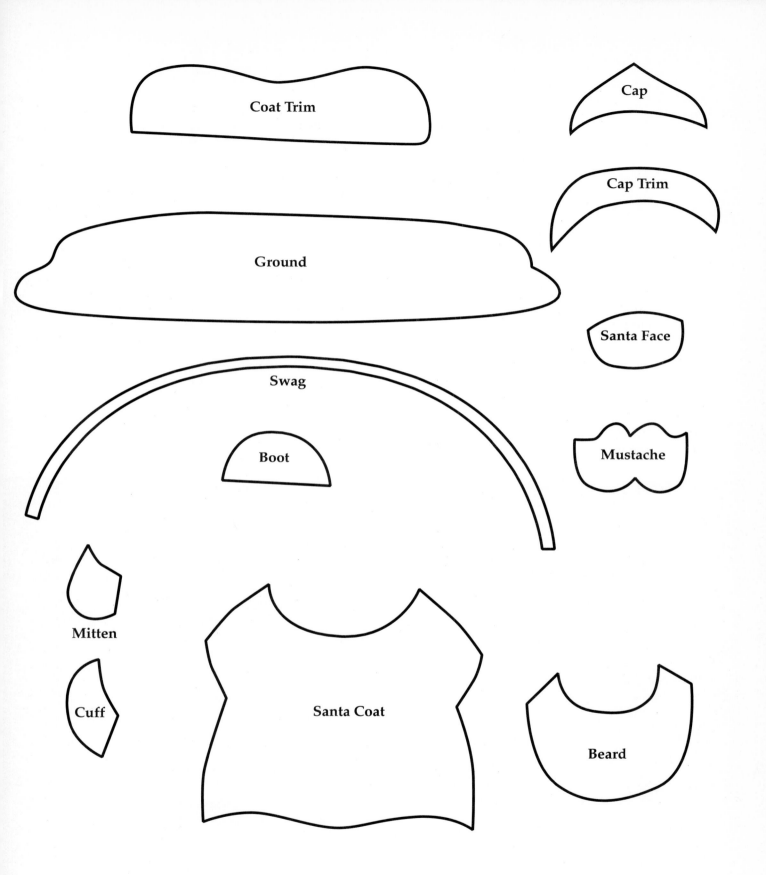

Coat Trim

Cap

Cap Trim

Ground

Santa Face

Swag

Mustache

Boot

Mitten

Cuff

Santa Coat

Beard

GENERAL INSTRUCTIONS

Complete instructions are given for making each of the quilts and other projects shown in this book. Skill levels indicated for quilts and wall hangings will help you choose the right project. To make your quilting easier and more enjoyable, we encourage you to read all of the general instructions, study the color photographs, and familiarize yourself with the individual project instructions before beginning a project.

QUILTING SUPPLIES

This list includes the basic tools needed for quick-method quiltmaking, plus additional supplies used for special techniques. Unless otherwise specified, all items can be found in your favorite fabric store or quilt shop.

Batting — Batting is most commonly available in polyester, cotton, or a polyester/cotton blend (see **Choosing and Preparing the Batting**, page 153).

Cutting mat — A cutting mat is a special mat designed to be used with a rotary cutter. A mat that measures approximately 18" x 24" is a good size for most cutting.

Eraser — A soft white fabric eraser or white art eraser may be used to remove pencil marks from fabric. Do not use a colored eraser, as the dye may discolor fabric.

Freezer Paper — This heavy white paper has a wax coating on one side that will adhere temporarily to fabric when applied with a dry iron.

Iron — An iron with both steam and dry settings and a smooth, clean soleplate is necessary for proper pressing.

Marking tools — There are many different marking tools available (see **Marking Quilting Lines**, page 152). A silver quilter's pencil is a good marker for both light and dark fabrics.

Masking tape — Two widths of masking tape, 1"w and ¹⁄₄"w, are helpful when quilting. The 1"w tape is used to secure the backing fabric to a flat surface when layering the quilt. The ¹⁄₄"w tape may be used as a guide when outline quilting.

Needles — Two types of needles are used for hand sewing: *Betweens*, used for quilting, are short and strong for stitching through layered fabric and batting. *Sharps* are longer, thinner needles used for basting, appliqué, and other hand sewing. For *sewing machine needles*, we recommend size 10 to 14 or 70 to 90 universal (sharp-pointed) needles.

Paper-backed fusible web — This iron-on adhesive with paper backing is used to secure fabric cutouts to another fabric when appliquéing. If the cutouts will be stitched in place, purchase the lighter weight web. A heavier weight web is used for appliqués that are fused in place with no stitching.

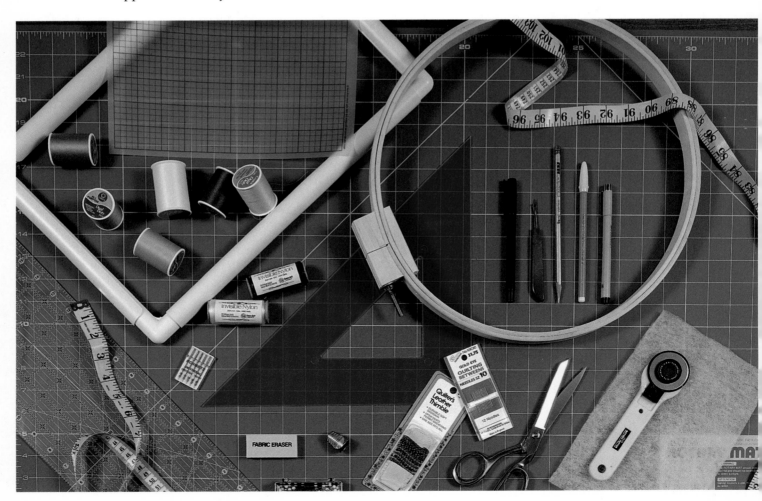

Permanent fine-point pen — A permanent pen is used to mark templates and stencils and to sign and date quilts. Test pen on fabric to make sure it will not bleed or wash out.

Pins — Straight pins made especially for quilting are extra long with large, round heads. Glass head pins will stand up to occasional contact with a hot iron. Some quilters prefer extra-fine dressmaker's silk pins. If you are machine quilting, you will need a large supply of 1" long (size 01) rust-proof safety pins for pin-basting.

Quilting hoop or frame — Quilting hoops and frames are designed to hold the 3 layers of a quilt together securely while you quilt. Many different types and sizes are available, including round and oval wooden hoops, frames made of rigid plastic pipe, and large floor frames made of either material. A 14" or 16" hoop allows you to quilt in your lap and makes your quilting portable.

Rotary cutter — The rotary cutter is the essential tool for quick-method quilting techniques. The cutter consists of a round, sharp blade mounted on a handle with a retractable blade guard for safety. It should be used only with a cutting mat and rotary cutting ruler. Two sizes are generally available; we recommend the larger (45 mm) size.

Rotary cutting ruler — A rotary cutting ruler is a thick, clear acrylic ruler made specifically for use with a rotary cutter. It should have accurate 1/8" crosswise and lengthwise markings and markings for 45° and 60° angles. A 6" x 24" ruler is a good size for most cutting. An additional 6" x 12" ruler or 12½" square ruler is helpful when cutting wider pieces. Many specialty rulers are available that make specific cutting tasks faster and easier.

Scissors — Although most fabric cutting will be done with a rotary cutter, sharp, high-quality scissors are still needed for some cutting. A separate pair of scissors for cutting paper and plastic is recommended. Smaller scissors are handy for clipping threads.

Seam ripper — A seam ripper with a fine point is useful for removing stitching.

Sewing machine — A sewing machine that produces a good, even straight stitch is all that is necessary for most quilting. Zigzag stitch capability is necessary for **Invisible Appliqué**, page 150. Clean and oil your machine often and keep the tension set properly.

Stabilizer — Commercially made non-woven material, or paper stabilizer, is placed behind background fabric when doing **Invisible Appliqué**, page 150, to provide a more stable stitching surface.

Tape measure — A flexible 120" long tape measure is helpful for measuring a quilt top before adding borders.

Template material — Sheets of translucent plastic, often pre-marked with a grid, are made especially for making templates and quilting stencils.

Thimble — A thimble is necessary when hand quilting. Thimbles are available in metal, plastic, or leather and in many sizes and styles. Choose a thimble that fits well and is comfortable.

Thread — Several types of thread are used for quiltmaking: *General-purpose* sewing thread is used for basting, piecing, and some appliquéing. Buy high-quality cotton or cotton-covered polyester thread in light and dark neutrals, such as ecru and grey, for your basic supplies. *Quilting* thread is stronger than general-purpose sewing thread, and some brands have a coating to make them slide more easily through the quilt layers. Some machine appliqué projects in this book use *transparent monofilament* (clear nylon) thread. Use a very fine (.004 mm), soft nylon thread that is not stiff or wiry. Choose clear nylon thread for white or light fabrics or smoke nylon thread for darker fabrics.

Triangle — A large plastic right-angle triangle (available in art and office supply stores) is useful in rotary cutting for making first cuts to "square up" raw edges of fabric and for checking to see that cuts remain at right angles to the fold.

Walking foot — A walking foot, or even-feed foot, is needed for straight-line machine quilting. This special foot will help all 3 layers of the quilt move at the same rate over the feed dogs to provide a smoother quilted project.

FABRICS

SELECTING FABRICS

Choose high-quality, medium-weight, 100% cotton fabrics such as broadcloth or calico. All-cotton fabrics hold a crease better, fray less, and are easier to quilt than cotton/polyester blends. All the fabrics for a quilt should be of comparable weight and weave. Check the end of the fabric bolt for fiber content and width.

The yardage requirements listed for each project are based on 45"-wide fabric with a "usable" width of 42" after shrinkage and trimming selvages. Your actual usable width will probably vary slightly from fabric to fabric. Though most fabrics will yield 42" or more, if you find a fabric that you suspect will yield a narrower usable width, you will need to purchase additional yardage to compensate. Our recommended yardage lengths should be adequate for occasional resquaring of fabric when many cuts are required, but it never hurts to buy a little more fabric for insurance against a narrower usable width, the occasional cutting error, or to have on hand for making coordinating projects.

PREPARING FABRICS

All fabrics should be washed, dried, and pressed before cutting.

1. To check colorfastness before washing, cut a small piece of the fabric and place in a glass of hot water with a little detergent. Leave fabric in the water for a few minutes. Remove from water and blot fabric with white paper towels. If any color bleeds onto the towels, wash the fabric separately with warm water and detergent and then rinse until the water runs clear. If fabric continues to bleed, choose another fabric.

2. Unfold yardage and separate fabrics by color. To help reduce raveling, use scissors to snip a small triangle from each corner of your fabric pieces. Machine wash fabrics in warm water with a small amount of mild laundry detergent. Do not use fabric softener. Rinse well and then dry fabrics in the dryer, checking long fabric lengths occasionally to make sure they are not tangling.

3. To make ironing easier, remove fabrics from dryer while they are slightly damp. Refold each fabric lengthwise (as it was on the bolt) with wrong sides together and matching selvages. If necessary, adjust slightly at selvages so that fold lays flat. Press each fabric with a steam iron set on "Cotton."

ROTARY CUTTING

*Based on the idea that you can easily cut strips of fabric and then cut those strips into smaller pieces, rotary cutting has brought speed and accuracy to quiltmaking. Observe safety precautions when using the rotary cutter since it is extremely sharp. Develop a habit of retracting the blade guard **just before** making a cut and closing it **immediately afterward**, before laying down the cutter.*

1. Follow **Preparing Fabrics**, page 145, to wash, dry, and press fabrics.
2. Cut all strips from the selvage-to-selvage width of the fabric unless otherwise indicated. Place fabric on the cutting mat, as shown in **Fig. 1**, with the fold of the fabric toward you. To straighten the uneven fabric edge, make the first "squaring up" cut by placing the right edge of the rotary cutting ruler over the left raw edge of the fabric. Place right-angle triangle (or another rotary cutting ruler) with the lower edge carefully aligned with the fold and the left edge against the ruler (**Fig. 1**). Hold the ruler firmly with your left hand, placing your little finger off the left edge to anchor the ruler. Remove the triangle, pick up the rotary cutter, and retract the blade guard. Using a smooth, downward motion, make the cut by running the blade of the rotary cutter firmly along the right edge of the ruler (**Fig. 2**). **Always** cut in a direction **away** from your body and **immediately** close the blade guard after each cut.

Fig. 1

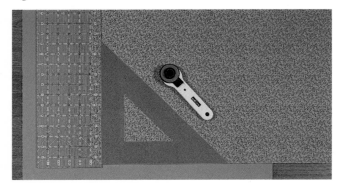

Fig. 2

3. To cut each of the strips required for a project, place the ruler over the cut edge of the fabric, aligning desired marking on the ruler with the cut edge (**Fig. 3**); make the cut. When cutting several strips from a single piece of fabric, it is important to occasionally use the ruler and triangle to ensure that cuts are still at a perfect right angle to the fold. If not, repeat Step 2 to straighten.

Fig. 3

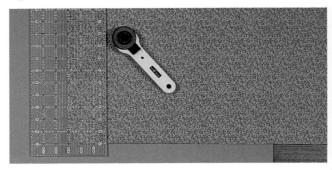

4. To square up selvage ends of a strip before cutting pieces, refer to **Fig. 4** and place folded strip on mat with selvage ends to your right. Aligning a horizontal marking on ruler with 1 long edge of strip, use rotary cutter to trim off selvage to make end of strip square and even (**Fig. 4**). Turn strip (or entire mat) so that cut end is to your left before making subsequent cuts.

Fig. 4

5. Pieces such as rectangles and squares can now be cut from strips. (Cutting other shapes, such as diamonds, is discussed in individual project instructions.) Usually strips remain folded, and pieces are cut in pairs after ends of strips are squared up. To cut squares or rectangles from a strip, place ruler over left end of strip, aligning desired marking on ruler with cut end of strip. To ensure perfectly square cuts, align a horizontal marking on ruler with 1 long edge of strip (**Fig. 5**) before making the cut.

Fig. 5

6. To cut 2 triangles from a square, cut square the size indicated in the project instructions. Cut square once diagonally to make 2 triangles (**Fig. 6**).

Fig. 6

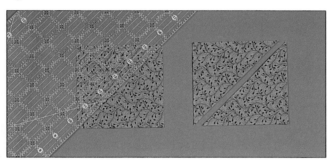

7. To cut 4 triangles from a square, cut square the size indicated in the project instructions. Cut square twice diagonally to make 4 triangles (**Fig. 7**). You may find it helpful to use a small rotary cutting mat so that the mat can be turned to make second cut without disturbing fabric pieces.

Fig. 7

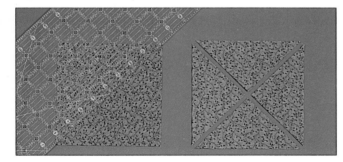

8. After some practice, you may want to try stacking up to 6 fabric layers when making cuts. When stacking strips, match long cut edges and follow Step 4 to square up ends of strip stack. Carefully turn stack (or entire mat) so that squared-up ends are to your left before making subsequent cuts. After cutting, check accuracy of pieces. Some shapes, such as diamonds, are more difficult to cut accurately in stacks.

9. In some cases, strips will be sewn together into strip sets before being cut into smaller units. When cutting a strip set, align a seam in strip set with a horizontal marking on the ruler to maintain square cuts (**Fig. 8**). We do not recommend stacking strip sets for rotary cutting.

Fig. 8

10. Most borders for quilts in this book are cut along the more stable lengthwise grain to minimize wavy edges caused by stretching. To remove selvages before cutting lengthwise strips, place fabric on mat with selvages to your left and squared-up end at bottom of mat. Placing ruler over selvage and using squared-up edge instead of fold, follow Step 2 to cut away selvages as you did raw edges (**Fig. 9**). After making a cut the length of the mat, move the next section of fabric to be cut onto the mat. Repeat until you have removed selvages from required length of fabric.

Fig. 9

11. After removing selvages, place ruler over left edge of fabric, aligning desired marking on ruler with cut edge of fabric. Make cuts as in Step 3. After each cut, move next section of fabric onto mat as in Step 10.

TEMPLATE CUTTING

Our full-sized piecing template patterns have 2 lines – a solid cutting line and a dashed line showing the ¼" seam allowance. Patterns for appliqué templates do not include seam allowances.

1. To make a template from a pattern, use a permanent fine-point pen to carefully trace pattern onto template plastic, making sure to transfer all alignment and grain line markings. Cut out template along inner edge of drawn line. Check template against original pattern for accuracy.

2. To use a template, place template on wrong side of fabric (unless otherwise indicated), aligning grain line on template with straight grain of fabric. Use a sharp fabric-marking pencil to draw around template. Transfer all alignment markings to fabric. Cut out fabric piece using scissors or rotary cutting equipment.

PIECING AND PRESSING

Precise cutting, followed by accurate piecing and careful pressing, will ensure that all the pieces of your quilt top fit together well.

PIECING

Set sewing machine stitch length for approximately 11 stitches per inch. Use a new, sharp needle suited for medium-weight woven fabric.

Use a neutral-colored general-purpose sewing thread (not quilting thread) in the needle and in the bobbin. Stitch first on a scrap of fabric to check upper and bobbin thread tension; make any necessary adjustments.

For good results, it is **essential** that you stitch with an **accurate ¼" seam allowance**. On many sewing machines, the measurement from the needle to the outer edge of the presser foot is ¼". If this is the case with your machine, the presser foot is your best guide. If not, measure ¼" from the needle and mark with a piece of masking tape. Special presser feet that are exactly ¼" wide are also available for most sewing machines.

When piecing, **always** place pieces **right sides together** and **match raw edges**; pin if necessary. (If using straight pins, remove the pins just before they reach the sewing machine needle.)

Chain Piecing

Chain piecing whenever possible will make your work go faster and will usually result in more accurate piecing. Stack the pieces you will be sewing beside your machine in the order you will need them and in a position that will allow you to easily pick them up. Pick up each pair of pieces, carefully place them together as they will be sewn, and feed them into the machine one after the other. Stop between each pair only long enough to pick up the next, and don't cut thread between pairs (**Fig. 10**). After all pieces are sewn, cut threads, press, and go on to the next step, chain piecing when possible.

Fig. 10

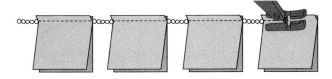

Sewing Across Seam Intersections

When sewing across the intersection of 2 seams, place pieces right sides together and match seams exactly, making sure seam allowances are pressed in opposite directions (**Fig. 11**). To prevent fabric from shifting, you may wish to pin in place.

Fig. 11

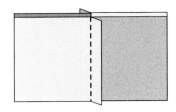

Sewing Sharp Points

To ensure sharp points when joining triangular or diagonal pieces, stitch across the center of the "X" (shown in pink) formed on the wrong side by previous seams (**Fig. 12**).

Fig. 12

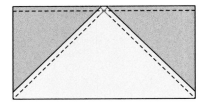

Making Triangle-Squares

The grid method for making triangle-squares is faster and more accurate than cutting and sewing individual triangles. Stitching before cutting the triangle-squares apart also prevents stretching of the bias edges.

1. Follow project instructions to cut rectangles or squares of fabric for making triangle-squares. Place the indicated pieces right sides together and press.
2. On the wrong side of the lighter fabric, draw a grid of squares similar to that shown in **Fig. 13**. The size and number of squares are given in the project instructions.

Fig. 13

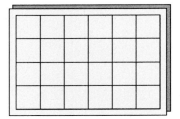

3. Following the example given in the project instructions, draw 1 diagonal line through each square in the grid (**Fig. 14**).

Fig. 14

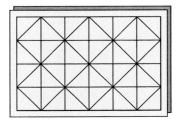

4. Stitch ¼" on each side of all diagonal lines. For accuracy, it may be helpful to first draw your stitching lines onto the fabric, especially if your presser foot is not your ¼" guide. In some cases, stitching may be done in a single continuous line. Project instructions include a diagram similar to **Fig. 15**, which shows stitching lines and the direction of the stitching.

Fig. 15

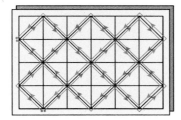

5. Use rotary cutter and ruler to cut along all drawn lines of the grid. Each square of the grid will yield 2 triangle-squares (**Fig. 16**).

Fig. 16

6. Carefully press triangle-squares open, pressing seam allowances toward darker fabric. Trim off points of seam allowances that extend beyond edges of triangle-square (see **Fig. 21**).

Working with Diamonds and Set-in Seams

Piecing diamonds and sewing set-in seams require special handling. For best results, carefully follow the steps below.

1. When sewing 2 diamonds together, place pieces right sides together, carefully matching edges; pin. Mark a small dot ¼" from corner of 1 piece as shown in **Fig. 17**. Stitch pieces together in the direction shown, stopping at center of dot and backstitching.

Fig. 17

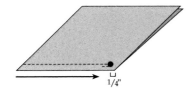

2. For best results, add side triangles, then corner squares to diamond sections. Mark corner of each piece to be set in with a small dot (**Fig. 18**).

Fig. 18

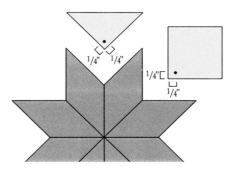

3. To sew first seam, match right sides and pin the triangle or square to the diamond on the left. Stitch seam from outer edge to the dot, backstitching at dot; clip threads (**Fig. 19**).

Fig. 19

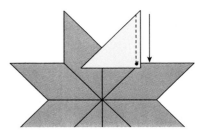

4. To sew the second seam, pivot the added triangle or square to match raw edges of next diamond. Beginning at dot, take 2 or 3 stitches, then backstitch, making sure not to backstitch into previous seam allowance. Continue stitching to outer edge (**Fig. 20**).

Fig. 20

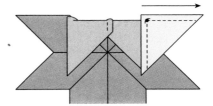

Trimming Seam Allowances

When sewing with diamond or triangle pieces, some seam allowances may extend beyond the edges of the sewn pieces. Trim away "dog ears" that extend beyond the edges of the sewn pieces (**Fig. 21**).

Fig. 21

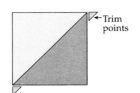

PRESSING

Use a steam iron set on "Cotton" for all pressing. Press as you sew, taking care to prevent small folds along seamlines. Seam allowances are almost always pressed to one side, usually toward the darker fabric. However, to reduce bulk it may occasionally be necessary to press seam allowances toward the lighter fabric or even to press them open. In order to prevent a dark fabric seam allowance from showing through a light fabric, trim the darker seam allowance slightly narrower than the lighter seam allowance. To press long seams, such as those in long strip sets, without curving or other distortion, lay strips across the width of the ironing board.

APPLIQUÉ

PREPARING FUSIBLE APPLIQUÉS

Patterns are printed in reverse to enable you to use our speedy method of preparing appliqués. White or light-colored fabrics may need to be lined with fusible interfacing before applying fusible web to prevent darker fabrics from showing through.

1. Place paper-backed fusible web, web side down, over appliqué pattern. Use a pencil to trace pattern onto paper side of web as many times as indicated in project instructions for a single fabric. Repeat for additional patterns and fabrics.
2. Follow manufacturer's instructions to fuse traced patterns to wrong side of fabrics. Do not remove paper backing. (*Note:* Some pieces may be given as measurements, such as a 2" x 4" rectangle, instead of drawn patterns. Fuse web to wrong side of fabrics indicated for these pieces.)
3. Use scissors to cut out appliqué pieces along traced lines; use rotary cutting equipment to cut out appliqué pieces given as measurements. Remove paper backing from all pieces.

INVISIBLE APPLIQUÉ

This machine appliqué method uses clear nylon thread to secure the appliqué pieces. Transparent monofilament (clear nylon) thread is available in 2 colors: clear and smoke. Use clear on white or very light fabrics and smoke on darker colors.

1. Referring to diagram and/or photo, arrange prepared appliqués on the background fabric and follow manufacturer's instructions to fuse in place.
2. Pin a stabilizer, such as paper or any of the commercially available products, on wrong side of background fabric before stitching appliqués in place.
3. Thread sewing machine with transparent monofilament thread; use general-purpose thread that matches background fabric in bobbin.
4. Set sewing machine for a very narrow (approximately 1/16") zigzag stitch and a short stitch length. You may find that loosening the top tension slightly will yield a smoother stitch.
5. Begin by stitching 2 or 3 stitches in place (drop feed dogs or set stitch length at 0) to anchor thread. Most of the zigzag stitch should be done on the appliqué with the right edges of the stitch falling at the very outside edge of the appliqué. Stitch over all exposed raw edges of appliqué pieces.

6. (*Note:* Dots on **Figs. 22 - 27** indicate where to leave needle in fabric when pivoting.) For **outside corners**, stitch just past the corner, stopping with the needle in **background** fabric (**Fig. 22**). Raise presser foot. Pivot project, lower presser foot, and stitch adjacent side (**Fig. 23**).

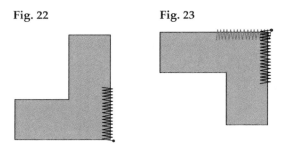

Fig. 22   **Fig. 23**

7. For **inside corners**, stitch just past the corner, stopping with the needle in **appliqué** fabric (**Fig. 24**). Raise presser foot. Pivot project, lower presser foot, and stitch adjacent side (**Fig. 25**).

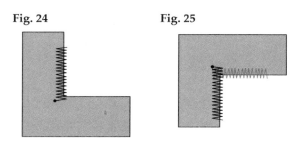

Fig. 24   **Fig. 25**

8. When stitching **outside** curves, stop with needle in **background** fabric. Raise presser foot and pivot project as needed. Lower presser foot and continue stitching, pivoting as often as necessary to follow curve (**Fig. 26**).

Fig. 26

9. When stitching **inside** curves, stop with needle in **appliqué** fabric. Raise presser foot and pivot project as needed. Lower presser foot and continue stitching, pivoting as often as necessary to follow curve (**Fig. 27**).

Fig. 27

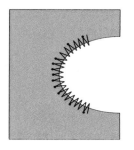

10. Do not backstitch at end of stitching. Pull threads to wrong side of background fabric; knot thread and trim ends.
11. Carefully tear away stabilizer.

HAND APPLIQUÉ

*In this traditional hand appliqué method, the needle is used to turn the seam allowance under as you sew the appliqué to the background fabric using a **Blind Stitch**, page 158.*

1. Place template on right side of appliqué fabric. Use a pencil to lightly draw around template, leaving at least 1/2" between shapes; repeat for number of shapes specified in project instructions.
2. Cut out shapes approximately 3/16" outside drawn line. Clip inside curves and points up to, but not through, drawn line. Arrange shapes on background fabric and pin or baste in place.
3. Thread a sharps needle with a single strand of general purpose sewing thread; knot one end.
4. For each appliqué shape, begin on as straight an edge as possible and turn a small section of seam allowance to wrong side with needle, concealing drawn line. Use blind stitch to sew appliqué to background, turning under edge and stitching as you continue around shape. Do not turn under or stitch seam allowances that will be covered by other appliqué pieces.
5. Follow **Cutting Away Fabric Behind Appliqués** to reduce bulk.

CUTTING AWAY FABRIC BEHIND APPLIQUÉS

Hand quilting an appliquéd block will be easier if you are stitching through as few layers as possible. For this reason, or just to reduce bulk in your quilt, you may wish to cut away the background fabric behind appliqués. After stitching appliqués in place, turn block over and use sharp scissors or specially designed appliqué scissors to trim away background fabric approximately 3/16" from stitching line. Take care not to cut appliqué fabric or stitches.

BORDERS

Borders cut along the lengthwise grain will lay flatter than borders cut along the crosswise grain. In most cases, our instructions for cutting borders for bed-sized quilts include an extra 2" at each end for "insurance"; borders will be trimmed after measuring completed center section of quilt top.

ADDING SQUARED BORDERS

1. Mark the center of each edge of quilt top.
2. Squared borders are usually added to top and bottom, then side edges of the center section of a quilt top. To add top and bottom borders, measure across center of quilt top to determine length of borders (**Fig. 28**). Trim top and bottom borders to the determined length.

Fig. 28

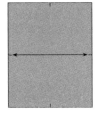

3. Mark center of 1 long edge of top border. Matching center marks and raw edges, pin border to quilt top, easing in any fullness; stitch. Repeat for bottom border.
4. Measure center of quilt top, including attached borders, to determine length of side borders. Trim side borders to the determined length. Repeat Step 3 to add borders to quilt top (**Fig. 29**).

Fig. 29

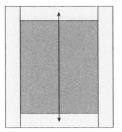

ADDING MITERED BORDERS

1. Mark the center of each edge of quilt top.
2. Mark center of 1 long edge of top border. Measure across center of quilt top (see **Fig. 28**). Matching center marks and raw edges, pin border to center of quilt top edge. Beginning at center of border, measure 1/2 the width of the quilt top in both directions and mark. Match marks on border with corners of quilt top and pin. Easing in any fullness, pin border to quilt top between center and corners. Sew border to quilt top, beginning and ending seams **exactly** 1/4" from each corner of quilt top and backstitching at beginning and end of stitching (**Fig. 30**).

Fig. 30

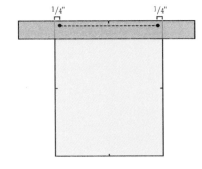

3. Repeat Step 2 to sew bottom, then side borders, to center section of quilt top. To temporarily move first 2 borders out of the way, fold and pin ends as shown in **Fig. 31**.

Fig. 31

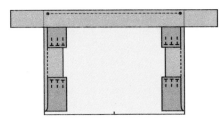

4. Fold 1 corner of quilt top diagonally with right sides together and matching edges. Use ruler to mark stitching line as shown in **Fig. 32**. Pin borders together along drawn line. Sew on drawn line, backstitching at beginning and end of stitching (**Fig. 33**).

Fig. 32 **Fig. 33**

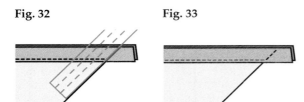

5. Turn mitered corner right side up. Check to make sure corner will lie flat with no gaps or puckers.
6. Trim seam allowance to ¼"; press to 1 side.
7. Repeat Steps 4 - 6 to miter each remaining corner.

QUILTING

*Quilting holds the 3 layers (top, batting, and backing) of the quilt together and can be done by hand or machine. Our project instructions tell you which method is used on each project and show quilting diagrams that can be used as suggestions for marking quilting designs. Because marking, layering, and quilting are interrelated and may be done in different orders depending on circumstances, please read the entire **Quilting** section, pages 152 - 154, before beginning the quilting process on your project.*

TYPES OF QUILTING

In the Ditch
Quilting very close to a seamline (**Fig. 34**) or appliqué (**Fig. 35**) is called "in the ditch" quilting. This type of quilting does not need to be marked and is indicated on our quilting diagrams with blue lines close to seamlines. When quilting in the ditch, quilt on the side **opposite** the seam allowance.

Fig. 34 **Fig. 35**

 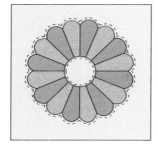

Outline Quilting
Quilting approximately ¼" from a seam or appliqué is called "outline" quilting (**Fig. 36**). This type of quilting is indicated on our quilting diagrams by blue lines a short distance from seamlines. Outline quilting may be marked, or you may place ¼"w masking tape along seamlines and quilt along the opposite edge of the tape. (Do not leave tape on quilt longer than necessary, since it may leave an adhesive residue.)

Fig. 36

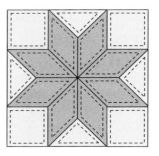

Ornamental Quilting
Quilting decorative lines or designs is called "ornamental" quilting (**Fig. 37**). Ornamental quilting is indicated on our quilting diagrams by blue lines. This type of quilting should be marked before you baste quilt layers together.

Fig. 37

MARKING QUILTING LINES
Fabric marking pencils, various types of chalk markers, and fabric marking pens with inks that disappear with exposure to air or water are readily available and work well for different applications. Lead pencils work well on light-colored fabric, but marks may be difficult to remove. White pencils work well on dark-colored fabric, and silver pencils show up well on many colors. Since chalk rubs off easily, it's a good choice if you are marking as you quilt. Fabric marking pens make more durable and visible markings, but the marks should be carefully removed according to manufacturer's instructions. Press down only as hard as necessary to make a visible line.

When you choose to mark your quilt, whether before or after the layers are basted together, is also a factor in deciding which marking tool to use. If you mark with chalk or a chalk pencil, handling the quilt during basting may rub off the markings. Intricate or ornamental designs may not be practical to mark as you quilt; mark these designs before basting using a more durable marker.

To choose marking tools, take all these factors into consideration and **test** different markers **on scrap fabric** until you find the one that gives the desired result.

USING QUILTING STENCILS
A wide variety of pre-cut quilting stencils and books of quilting patterns are available. Using a stencil makes it easier to mark intricate or repetitive designs on your quilt top.

1. To make a stencil from a pattern, center template plastic over pattern and use a permanent marker to trace pattern onto plastic.

Use a craft knife with a single or double blade to cut narrow slits along traced lines (**Fig. 38**).

Fig. 38

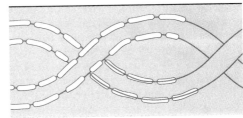

3. Use desired marking tool and stencil to mark quilting lines.

CHOOSING AND PREPARING THE BACKING

To allow for slight shifting of the quilt top during quilting, the backing should be approximately 4" larger on all sides for a bed-size quilt top or approximately 2" larger on all sides for a wall hanging. Yardage requirements listed for quilt backings are calculated for 45"w fabric. If you are making a bed-size quilt, using 90"w or 108"w fabric for the backing may eliminate the need for piecing. To piece a backing using 45"w fabric, use the following instructions.

1. Measure length and width of quilt top; add 8" (4" for a wall hanging) to each measurement.
2. If quilt top is 76"w or less, cut backing fabric into 2 lengths slightly longer than the determined **length** measurement. Trim selvages. Place lengths with right sides facing and sew long edges together, forming a tube (**Fig. 39**). Match seams and press along 1 fold (**Fig. 40**). Cut along pressed fold to form a single piece (**Fig. 41**).

Fig. 39   Fig. 40   Fig. 41

 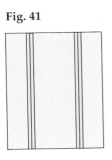

3. If quilt top is more than 76"w, cut backing fabric into 3 lengths slightly longer than the determined **width** measurement. Trim selvages. Sew long edges together to form a single piece.
4. Trim backing to correct size, if necessary, and press seam allowances open.

CHOOSING AND PREPARING THE BATTING

Choosing the right batting will make your quilting job easier. For fine hand quilting, choose a low-loft batting in any of the fiber types described here. Machine quilters will want to choose a low-loft batting that is all cotton or a cotton/polyester blend, because the cotton helps "grip" the layers of the quilt. If the quilt is to be tied, a high-loft batting, sometimes called extra-loft or fat batting, is a good choice.

Batting is available in many different fibers. Bonded polyester batting is one of the most popular batting types. It is treated with a protective coating to stabilize the fibers and to reduce "bearding," a process where batting fibers work their way through the quilt fabrics. Other batting options include cotton/polyester batting, which combines the best of both polyester and cotton battings; all-cotton batting, which must be quilted more closely than polyester batting; and wool and silk battings, which are generally more expensive and usually only dry-cleanable.

Whichever batting you choose, read the manufacturer's instructions closely for any special notes on care or preparation. When you're ready to use your chosen batting in a project, cut batting the same size as the prepared backing.

LAYERING THE QUILT

1. Examine wrong side of quilt top closely; trim any seam allowances and clip any threads that may show through the front of the quilt. Press quilt top.
2. If quilt top is to be marked before layering, mark quilting lines (see **Marking Quilting Lines**, page 152).
3. Place backing **wrong** side up on a flat surface. Use masking tape to tape edges of backing to surface. Place batting on top of backing fabric. Smooth batting gently, being careful not to stretch or tear. Center quilt top **right** side up on batting.
4. If hand quilting, begin in the center and work toward the outer edges to hand baste all layers together. Use long stitches and place basting lines approximately 4" apart (**Fig. 42**). Smooth fullness or wrinkles toward outer edges.

Fig. 42

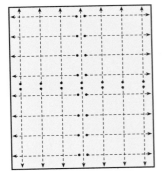

5. If machine quilting, use 1" rust-proof safety pins to "pin-baste" all layers together, spacing pins approximately 4" apart. Begin at the center and work toward the outer edges to secure all layers. If possible, place pins away from areas that will be quilted, although pins may be removed as needed when quilting.

HAND QUILTING

The quilting stitch is a basic running stitch that forms a broken line on the quilt top and backing. Stitches on the quilt top and backing should be straight and equal in length.

1. Secure center of quilt in hoop or frame. Check quilt top and backing to make sure they are smooth. To help prevent puckers, always begin quilting in the center of the quilt and work toward the outside edges.
2. Thread needle with an 18" - 20" length of quilting thread; knot 1 end. Using a thimble, insert needle into quilt top and batting approximately ½" from where you wish to begin quilting. Bring needle up at the point where you wish to begin (**Fig. 43**); when knot catches on quilt top, give thread a quick, short pull to "pop" knot through fabric into batting (**Fig. 44**).

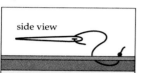

Fig. 43

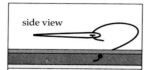

Fig. 44

3. Holding the needle with your sewing hand and placing your other hand underneath the quilt, use thimble to push the tip of the needle down through all layers. As soon as needle touches your finger underneath, use that finger to push the tip of the needle only back up through the layers to top of quilt. (The amount of the needle showing above the fabric determines the length of the quilting stitch.) Referring to **Fig. 45**, rock the needle up and down, taking 3 - 6 stitches before bringing the needle and thread completely through the layers. Check the back of the quilt to make sure stitches are going through all layers. When quilting through a seam allowance or quilting a curve or corner, you may need to take 1 stitch at a time.

Fig. 45

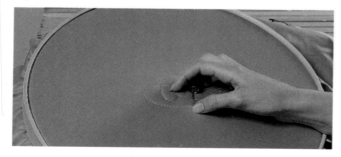

4. When you reach the end of your thread, knot thread close to the fabric and "pop" knot into batting; clip thread close to fabric.
5. Stop and move your hoop as often as necessary. You do not have to tie a knot every time you move your hoop; you may leave the thread dangling and pick it up again when you return to that part of the quilt.

MACHINE STIPPLE QUILTING
The term "stipple quilting" refers to extensive, closely spaced quilting, usually used to fill in background areas of pieced or appliquéd blocks. The machine-quilted projects in this book feature machine stipple quilting, which is indicated on our quilting diagrams by closely spaced meandering blue lines and does not need to be marked.

1. Wind your sewing machine bobbin with general-purpose thread that matches the quilt backing. Do not use quilting thread. Thread the needle of your machine with transparent monofilament thread if you want your quilting to blend with your quilt top fabrics. Use decorative thread, such as a metallic or contrasting-colored general-purpose thread, when you want the quilting lines to stand out.
2. For random stipple quilting, use a darning foot, drop or cover feed dogs, and set stitch length at zero. Stitch 2 or 3 stitches in place to lock thread. Place hands lightly on quilt on either side of darning foot.
3. Begin stitching in a meandering pattern (**Fig. 46**), guiding the quilt with your hands. The object is to make stitches of similar length and to not sew over previous stitching lines. The movement of your hands determines the stitch length; it takes practice to coordinate your hand motions and the pressure you put on the foot pedal, so go slowly at first.

Fig. 46

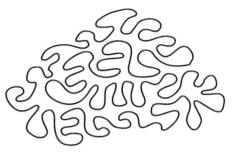

4. Continue machine quilting, filling in one open area of the quilt before moving on to another area and locking thread again at end of each line of stitching by sewing 2 or 3 stitches in place.

BINDING

Binding encloses the raw edges of your quilt. Because of its stretchiness, bias binding works well for binding projects with curves or rounded corners and tends to lie smooth and flat in any given circumstance. It is also more durable than other types of binding. Binding may also be cut from the straight lengthwise or crosswise grain of the fabric. You will find that straight-grain binding works well for projects with straight edges.

MAKING CONTINUOUS BIAS STRIP BINDING
Bias strips for binding can simply be cut and pieced to the desired length. However, when a long length of binding is needed, the "continuous" method is quick and accurate.

1. Cut a square from binding fabric the size indicated in the project instructions. Cut square in half diagonally to make 2 triangles.
2. With right sides together and using a ¼" seam allowance, sew triangles together (**Fig. 47**); press seam allowance open.

Fig. 47

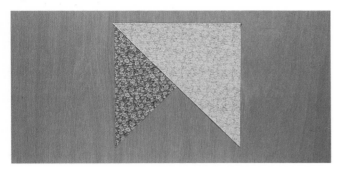

3. On wrong side of fabric, draw lines the width of the binding as specified in the project instructions, usually 2½" (**Fig. 48**). Cut off any remaining fabric less than this width.

Fig. 48

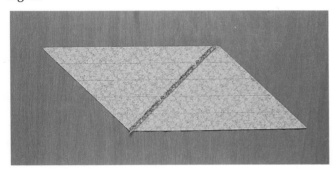

4. With right sides inside, bring short edges together to form a tube; match raw edges so that first drawn line of top section meets second drawn line of bottom section (**Fig. 49**).

Fig. 49

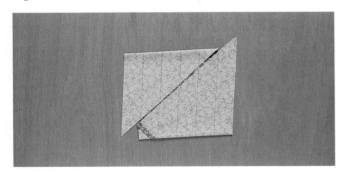

5. Carefully pin edges together by inserting pins through drawn lines at the point where drawn lines intersect, making sure the pins go through intersections on both sides. Using a ¼" seam allowance, sew edges together. Press seam allowance open.
6. To cut continuous strip, begin cutting along first drawn line (**Fig. 50**). Continue cutting along drawn line around tube.

Fig. 50

7. Trim ends of bias strip square.
8. Matching wrong sides and raw edges, press bias strip in half lengthwise to complete binding.

MAKING STRAIGHT-GRAIN BINDING

1. To determine length of strip needed if attaching binding with mitered corners, measure edges of the quilt and add 12".
2. To determine lengths of strips needed if attaching binding with overlapped corners, measure each edge of quilt; add 3" to each measurement.
3. Cut lengthwise or crosswise strips of binding fabric the determined length and the width called for in the project instructions. Strips may be pieced to achieve the necessary length.
4. Matching wrong sides and raw edges, press strip(s) in half lengthwise to complete binding.

ATTACHING BINDING WITH MITERED CORNERS

1. Press 1 end of binding diagonally (**Fig. 51**).

Fig. 51

2. Beginning with pressed end several inches from a corner, lay binding around quilt to make sure that seams in binding will not end up at a corner. Adjust placement if necessary. Matching raw edges of binding to raw edge of quilt top, pin binding to right side of quilt along 1 edge.
3. When you reach the first corner, mark ¼" from corner of quilt top (**Fig. 52**).

Fig. 52

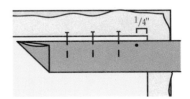

155

4. Using a ¼" seam allowance, sew binding to quilt, backstitching at beginning of stitching and when you reach the mark (**Fig. 53**). Lift needle out of fabric and clip thread.

Fig. 53

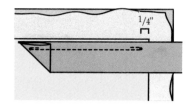

5. Fold binding as shown in **Figs. 54** and **55** and pin binding to adjacent side, matching raw edges. When you reach the next corner, mark ¼" from edge of quilt top.

Fig. 54   **Fig. 55**

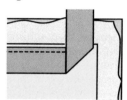 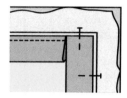

6. Backstitching at edge of quilt top, sew pinned binding to quilt (**Fig. 56**); backstitch when you reach the next mark. Lift needle out of fabric and clip thread.

Fig. 56

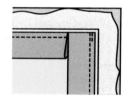

7. Repeat Steps 5 and 6 to continue sewing binding to quilt until binding overlaps beginning end by approximately 2". Trim excess binding.
8. If using 2½"w binding (finished size ½"), trim backing and batting a scant ¼" larger than quilt top so that batting and backing will fill the binding when it is folded over to the quilt backing. If using narrower binding, trim backing and batting even with edges of quilt top.
9. On 1 edge of quilt, fold binding over to quilt backing and pin pressed edge in place, covering stitching line (**Fig. 57**). On adjacent side, fold binding over, forming a mitered corner (**Fig. 58**). Repeat to pin remainder of binding in place.

Fig. 57   **Fig. 58**

10. Blindstitch binding to backing, taking care not to stitch through to front of quilt.

ATTACHING BINDING WITH OVERLAPPED CORNERS

1. Matching raw edges and using a ¼" seam allowance, sew a length of binding to top and bottom edges on right side of quilt.
2. If using 2½"w binding (finished size ½"), trim backing and batting from top and bottom edges a scant ¼" larger than quilt top so that batting and backing will fill the binding when it is folded over to the quilt backing. If using narrower binding, trim backing and batting even with edges of quilt top.
3. Trim ends of top and bottom binding even with edges of quilt top. Fold binding over to quilt backing and pin pressed edges in place, covering stitching line (**Fig. 59**); blindstitch binding to backing.

Fig. 59

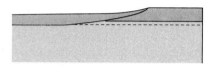

4. Leaving approximately 1½" of binding at each end, stitch a length of binding to each side edge of quilt. Trim backing and batting as in Step 2.
5. Trim each end of binding ½" longer than bound edge. Fold each end of binding over to quilt backing (**Fig. 60**); pin in place. Fold binding over to quilt backing and blindstitch in place, taking care not to stitch through to front of quilt.

Fig. 60

MAKING A HANGING SLEEVE

Attaching a hanging sleeve to the back of your wall hanging or quilt before the binding is added allows you to display your completed project on a wall.

1. Measure the width of the wall hanging top and subtract 1". Cut a piece of fabric 7"w by the determined measurement.
2. Press short edges of fabric piece ¼" to wrong side; press edges ¼" to wrong side again and machine stitch in place.
3. Matching wrong sides, fold piece in half lengthwise to form a tube.
4. Follow project instructions to sew binding to quilt top and to trim backing and batting. Before blindstitching binding to backing, match raw edges and stitch hanging sleeve to center top edge on back of wall hanging.
5. Finish binding wall hanging, treating the hanging sleeve as part of the backing.
6. Blindstitch bottom of hanging sleeve to backing, taking care not to stitch through to front of quilt.
7. Insert dowel or slat into hanging sleeve.

SIGNING AND DATING YOUR QUILT

Your completed quilt is a work of art and should be signed and dated. There are many different ways to do this, and you should pick a method that reflects the style of the quilt, the occasion for which it was made, and your own particular talents.

The following suggestions may give you an idea for recording the history of your quilt for future generations.

- Embroider your name, the date, and any additional information on the quilt top or backing. You may choose floss colors that closely match the fabric you are working on, such as white floss on a white border, or contrasting colors may be used.
- Make a label from muslin and use a permanent marker to write your information. Your label may be as plain or as fancy as you wish. Stitch the label to the back of the quilt.
- Chart a cross-stitch label design that includes the information you wish and stitch it in colors that complement the quilt. Stitch the finished label to the quilt backing.

PILLOW FINISHING

Any quilt block may be made into a pillow. If desired, you may add welting and/or a ruffle to the pillow top before sewing the pillow top and back together.

ADDING WELTING TO PILLOW TOP

1. To make welting, use bias strip indicated in project instructions. (Or measure edges of pillow top and add 4". Measure circumference of cord and add 2". Cut a bias strip of fabric the determined measurement, piecing if necessary.)
2. Lay cord along center of bias strip on wrong side of fabric; fold strip over cord. Using a zipper foot, machine baste along length of strip close to cord. Trim seam allowance to the width you will use to sew pillow top and back together (see Step 2 of **Making the Pillow**).
3. Matching raw edges and beginning and ending 3" from ends of welting, baste welting to right side of pillow top. To make turning corners easier, clip seam allowance of welting at pillow top corners.
4. Remove approximately 3" of seam at 1 end of welting; fold fabric away from cord. Trim remaining end of welting so that cord ends meet exactly (**Fig. 61**).

Fig. 61

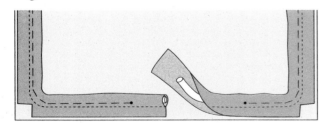

5. Fold short edge of welting fabric ½" to wrong side; fold fabric back over area where ends meet (**Fig. 62**).

Fig. 62

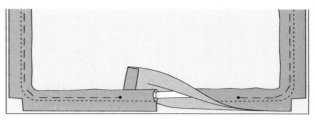

6. Baste remainder of welting to pillow top close to cord (**Fig. 63**).

Fig. 63

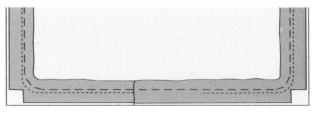

7. Follow **Making the Pillow** to complete pillow.

ADDING RUFFLE TO PILLOW TOP

1. To make ruffle, use fabric strip indicated in project instructions.
2. Matching right sides, use a ¼" seam allowance to sew short edges of ruffle together to form a large circle; press seam allowance open. To form ruffle, fold along length with wrong sides together and raw edges matching; press.
3. To gather ruffle, place quilting thread ¼" from raw edge of ruffle. Using a medium width zigzag stitch with medium stitch length, stitch over quilting thread, being careful not to catch quilting thread in stitching. Pull quilting thread, drawing up gathers to fit pillow top.
4. Matching raw edges, baste ruffle to right side of pillow top.
5. Follow **Making the Pillow** to complete pillow.

MAKING THE PILLOW

1. For pillow back, cut a piece of fabric the same size as pieced and quilted pillow top.
2. Place pillow back and pillow top right sides together. The seam allowance width you use will depend on the construction of the pillow top. If the pillow top has borders where the finished width of the border is not crucial, use a ½" seam allowance for durability. If the pillow top is pieced where a wider seam allowance would interfere with the design, use a ¼" seam allowance. Using the determined seam allowance (or stitching as close as possible to welting), sew pillow top and back together, leaving an opening at bottom edge for turning.
3. Turn pillow right side out, carefully pushing corners outward. Stuff with polyester fiberfill or pillow form and sew final closure by hand.

EMBROIDERY STITCHES

Straight Stitch

Come up at 1 and go down at 2 (**Fig. 64**). Length of stitches may be varied as desired.

Fig. 64

Stem Stitch

Come up at 1. Keeping thread below the stitching line, go down at 2 and come up at 3. Go down at 4 and come up at 5 (**Fig. 65**).

Fig. 65

Satin Stitch

Come up at 1; go down at 2 and come up at 3. Continue until area is filled (**Fig. 66**).

Fig. 66

Running Stitch

The running stitch consists of a series of straight stitches with the stitch length equal to the space between stitches (**Fig. 67**).

Fig. 67

Blanket Stitch

Come up at 1. Go down at 2 and come up at 3, keeping thread below point of needle (**Fig. 68**). Continue working as shown in **Fig. 69**.

Fig. 68

Fig. 69

Blindstitch

Come up at 1. Go down at 2 and come up at 3 (**Fig. 70**). Length of stitches may be varied as desired.

Fig. 70

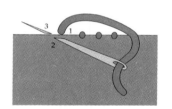

GLOSSARY

Appliqué — A cutout fabric shape that is secured to a larger background. Also refers to the technique of securing the cutout pieces.

Backing — The back or bottom layer of a quilt, sometimes called the "lining."

Backstitch — A reinforcing stitch taken at the beginning and end of a seam to secure stitches.

Basting — Large running stitches used to temporarily secure pieces or layers of fabric together. Basting is removed after permanent stitching.

Batting — The middle layer of a quilt that provides insulation and warmth as well as thickness.

Bias — The diagonal (45° for true bias) grain of fabric in relation to crosswise or lengthwise grain (see **Fig. 71**).

Binding — The fabric strip used to enclose the raw edges of the layered and quilted quilt. Also refers to the technique of finishing quilt edges in this way.

Blindstitch — A method of hand sewing that is nearly invisible.

Border — Strips of fabric that are used to frame a quilt top.

Chain piecing — A machine-piecing method consisting of joining pairs of pieces one after the other by feeding them through the sewing machine without cutting the thread between the pairs.

Grain — The direction of the threads in woven fabric. "Crosswise grain" refers to the threads running from selvage to selvage. "Lengthwise grain" refers to the threads running parallel to the selvages (**Fig. 71**).

Fig. 71

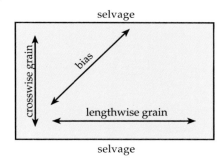

Machine baste — To baste using a sewing machine set at a long stitch length.

Miter — A method used to finish corners of quilt borders or bindings consisting of joining fabric pieces at a 45° angle.

Piecing — Sewing together the pieces of a quilt design to form a quilt block or an entire quilt top.

Pin basting — Using rust-proof safety pins to secure the layers of a quilt together prior to machine quilting.

Quilt block — Pieced or appliquéd sections that are sewn together to form a quilt top.

Quilt top — The decorative part of a quilt that is layered on top of the batting and backing.

Quilting — The stitching that holds together the 3 quilt layers (top, batting, and backing). Also refers to the entire process of making a quilt.

Sashing — Strips or blocks of fabric that separate individual blocks in a quilt top.

Seam allowance — The distance between the seam and the cut edge of the fabric. In quilting, the seam allowance is usually ¼".

Selvages — The 2 finished lengthwise edges of fabric (see **Fig. 71**). Selvages should be trimmed from fabric before cutting.

Set (or Setting) — The arrangement of the quilt blocks as they are sewn together to form the quilt top.

Setting squares — Squares of plain (unpieced) fabric set between pieced or appliquéd quilt blocks in a quilt top.

Setting triangles — Triangles of fabric used around the outside of a diagonally-set quilt top to fill in between outer squares and border or binding.

Stencil — A pattern used for marking quilting lines.

Straight grain — The crosswise or lengthwise grain of fabric (see **Fig. 71**). The lengthwise grain has the least amount of stretch.

Strip set — Two or more strips of fabric that are sewn together along the long edges and then cut apart across the width of the sewn strips to create smaller units.

Template — A pattern used for marking quilt pieces to be cut out.

Triangle-square — In piecing, 2 right triangles joined along their long sides to form a square with a diagonal seam (**Fig. 72**).

Fig. 72

Unit — A pieced section that is made as individual steps in the quilt construction process are completed. Units are usually combined to make blocks or other sections of the quilt top.

CREDITS

We want to extend a warm *thank you* to the generous people who allowed us to photograph our projects at their homes.

- *Garden Wedding Collection:*
  Dr. Dan and Sandra Cook
- *Scrappy Bear's Paw:* Carl and Monte Brunck
- *True Lover's Knot:* Duncan and Nancy Porter
- *Feathered Star Collection:*
  Charles and Peggy Mills
- *Castle in the Mountains Collection:*
  Ron and Becky Werle
- *Trip Around the World:*
  Ron and Becky Werle

- *Pansy Collection:*
  Dr. David and Linda Wardlaw
- *Amish Collection:* Duncan and Nancy Porter
- *Calico Courthouse Steps:*
  Dr. Dan and Sandra Cook
- *Clay's Choice Collection:*
  Carl and Monte Brunck
- *Lone Star Log Cabin:*
  Dr. Dan and Sandra Cook
- *Friendship Collection:*
  Dr. Dan and Sandra Cook

The following projects are from the collection of Bryce and Donna Hamilton, Minneapolis, Minnesota: Scrappy Bear's Paw Quilt, page 40; Trip Around the World Quilt, page 58; Crosses and Losses Quilt, page 80; and Lone Star Log Cabin Quilt, page 112.

The following projects were designed by Sharon LoMonaco: Pansy Wall Hanging, page 66; Bouquet Pillow, Pansy Valance, and Curtain Tiebacks, page 67; and Clay's Choice Quilt, page 94.

The Castle in the Mountains Wall Hanging, page 49, was based on a pattern by Kathy Love, Love Quilt Patterns.

Thanks also go to Viking Husqvarna Sewing Machine Company of Cleveland, Ohio, for providing the sewing machines used to make many of the projects in this book.

To Magna IV Color Imaging of Little Rock, Arkansas, we say thank you for the superb color reproduction and excellent pre-press preparation.

We especially want to thank photographers Mark Mathews, Larry Pennington, Karen Shirey, and Ken West of Peerless Photography, Little Rock, Arkansas, and Jerry R. Davis of Jerry Davis Photography, Little Rock, Arkansas, for their time, patience, and excellent work.

We extend a sincere *thank you* to all the people who assisted in making and testing the projects in this book: Karen Call, Deborah B. Chance, Valerie Doiel, Cheryl Farmer, Wanda Fite, Patricia Galas, Grace Grame, Judith Hassed, Barbara Herring, Lea Hyland, Kimberly James, Liz Lane, Barbara Middleton, Linda Nelson, Ruby Solida, Glenda Taylor, Jennifer M. Vechik; the Gardner Memorial United Methodist Church Quilters, North Little Rock, Arkansas: Elois Allain, Vina Lindermon, Fredda McBride, Betty Smith, Esther Starkey, Maxine Bramblett, Leon Dickey, and Grace Brooks; and the Mabelvale United Methodist Church Quilters, Mabelvale, Arkansas: Sunny Ball, Dorothy Clement, Mary Sue Meyer, Carolyn Moseley, Mickey Riddle, and Jacquelynn Spann.